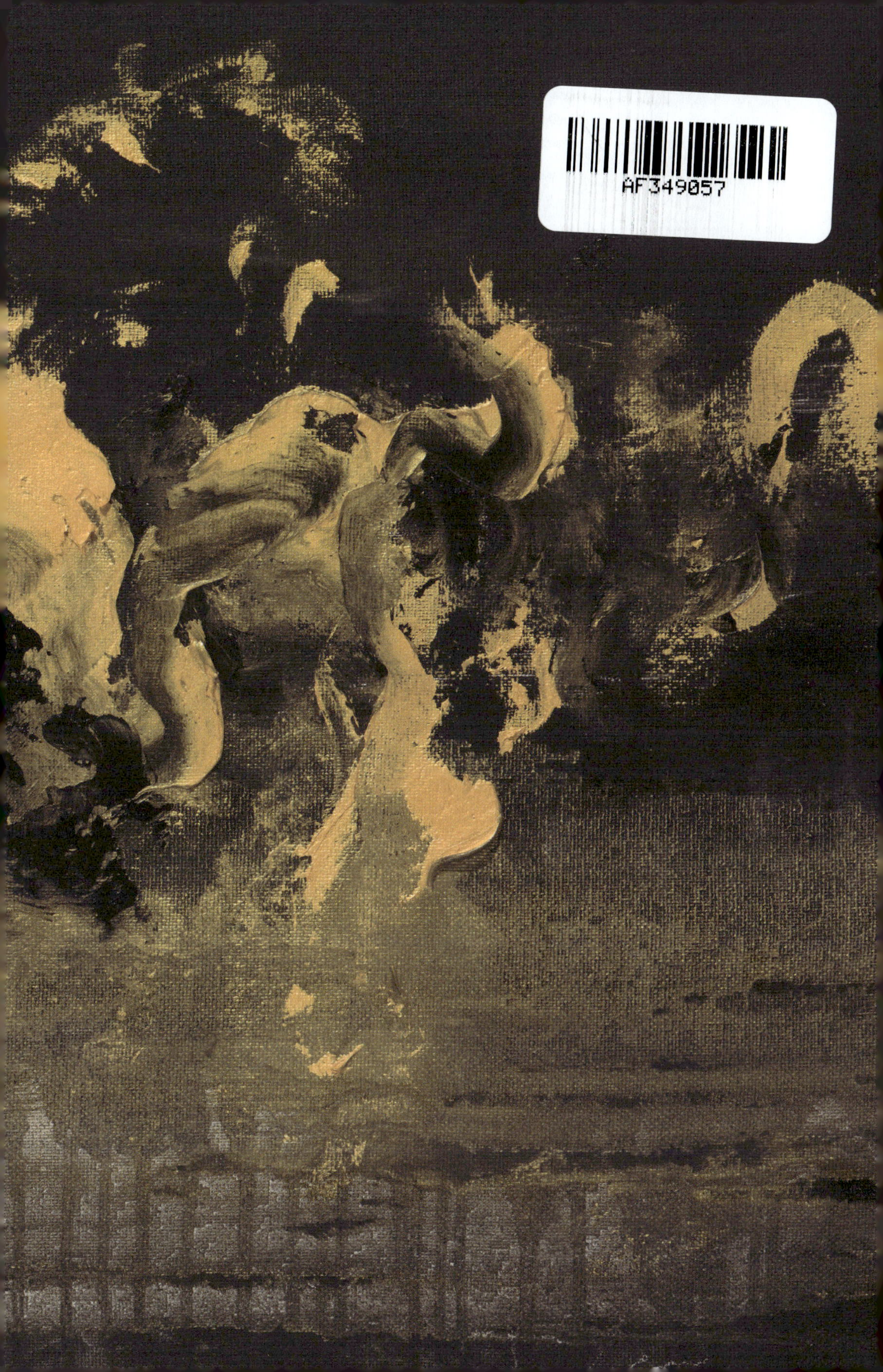
AF349057

Maggi Hambling

Nightingale night

Maggi Hambling

Nightingale night

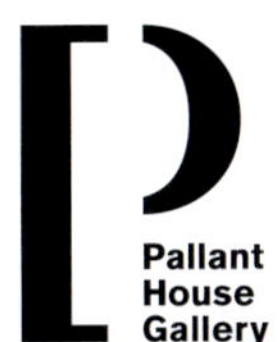

Pallant House Gallery

Maggi Hambling: Nightingale night

First published in the United Kingdom in 2024 by
Pallant House Gallery on the occasion of the exhibition
Maggi Hambling: Nightingale night
(9 November 2024–27 April 2025)

Photography:
Paintings, pp.7, 16 and 19 © Douglas Atfield
Back cover, pp.9, 36–7, 38, 43–4 and 46 © Simon Martin, 2024
pp.40–2 © Ollie Denton, 2023–4, courtesy Sam Lee

Text and lyrics:
Foreword © Simon Martin, 2024
A Savage Kind of Brilliance © James Cahill, 2024.
Reprinted by permission of the author c/o Blake Friedmann Literary Agency Ltd.
Decorations of Silence © Sam Lee, 2024
The Nightingale © PJ Harvey
Night of the Lotus Eaters. Written by Nick Cave
© BMG Music Publishing Ltd, reproduced with kind permission
Night of the Lotus Eaters
Words and Music by Nick Cave and Warren Ellis
Copyright © 2008 BMG Rights Management (UK) Limited and Mute Song Ltd.
All Rights for BMG Rights Management (UK) Limited
Administered by BMG Rights Management (US) LLC
All Rights Reserved Used by Permission
Reprinted by Permission of Hal Leonard Europe Ltd.

Pallant House Gallery
8–9 North Pallant
Chichester
West Sussex
PO19 1TJ
Tel: +44(0)1243 774557
info@pallant.org.uk
www.pallant.org.uk

British Library Cataloguing-in-Publications Data
A catalogue record for this book is available from the British Library

ISBN: 978-1-869827-66-3
Library of Congress Control Number: 2024937299

Copy edited by Susannah Worth
Publication Manager: Harriet Olsen
Designed by Webb & Webb Design Ltd
Set in Garamond

Printed and bound in the UK by Gomer Press Ltd

Distributed for Pallant House Gallery by Yale University Press,
New Haven and London

ENDPAPERS
Nightingale night VII, 2023 (detail)
Oil on canvas, 40.6 x 61.0 cm

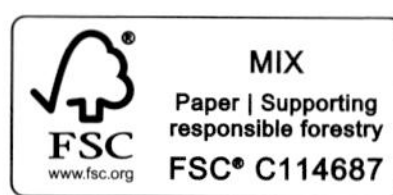

Contents

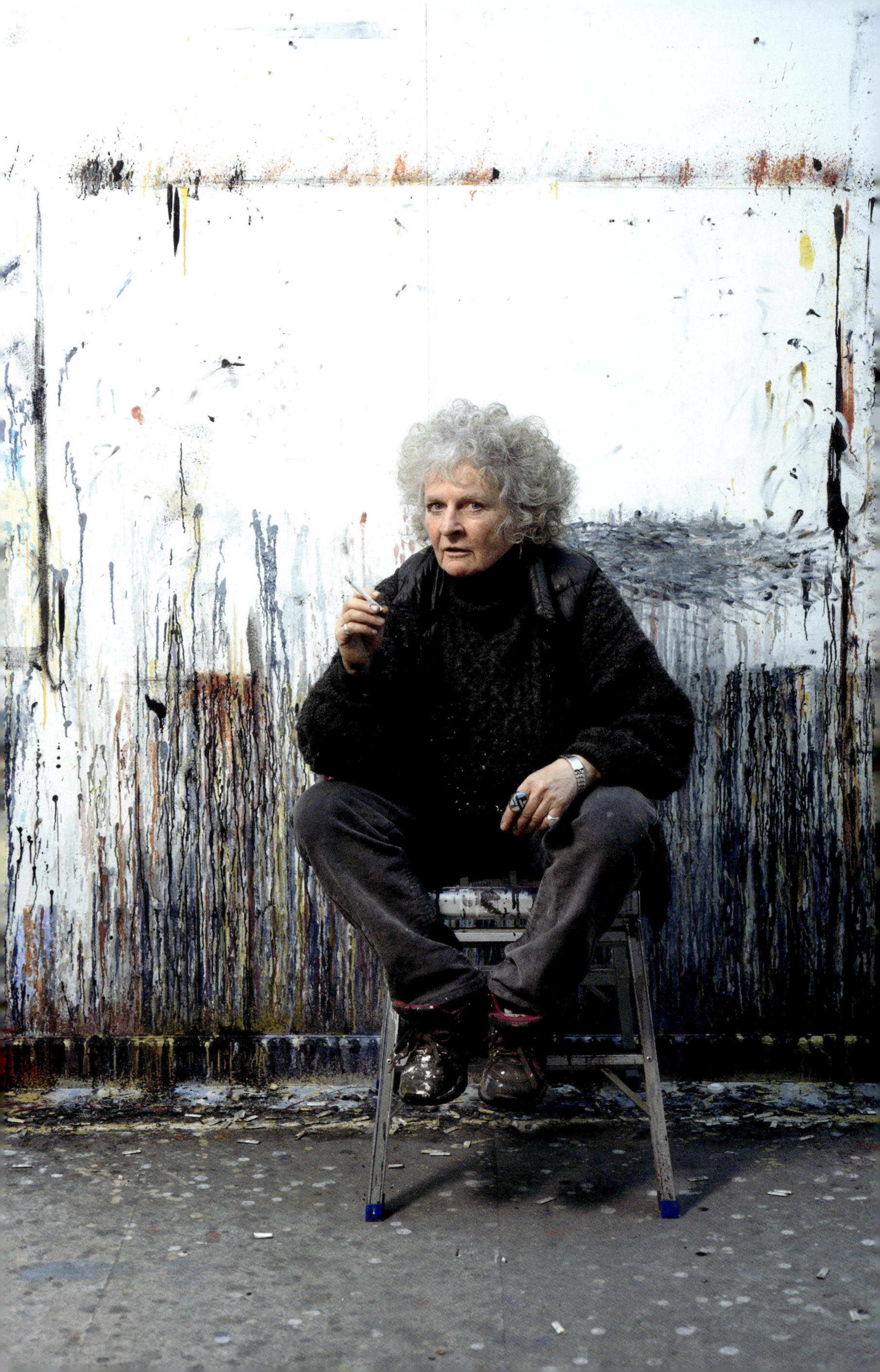

Foreword

Simon Martin, *Director Pallant House Gallery*

Maggi Hambling scarcely needs any introduction. She is one of the most legendary figures currently working in the British art world.

Talking with an artist friend recently, I was struck by their observation of how intensely Maggi feels her subject matter. Whether in paintings and drawings of friends and lovers, evocations of the crash of the waves in the North Sea, or sculptures honouring musical and literary figures such as Benjamin Britten, Oscar Wilde and Mary Wollstonecraft, that intensity of feeling is palpable. It is a quality that draws us into her work and enables us to share in those feelings.

I first met Maggi 15 years ago when I included her in an exhibition of East Anglian artists at Salthouse in North Norfolk. She invited me to her studio in Suffolk to choose a painting of the North Sea for the exhibition, and I'll never forget that first encounter. I must admit that I was rather terrified, but watching her paint in the studio, her hair somehow reminding me of the tempestuous sea, I knew that I was in the presence of an extraordinary artist. Over the years since, we've seen each other relatively frequently, not least at an in-conversation when audience members called me 'brave', much to Maggi's amusement.

In 2020, Maggi was one of 32 contemporary artists, including John Akomfrah, Cecily Brown, Damien Hirst, Grayson Perry and Rachel Whiteread, who generously contributed a miniature artwork to a model art gallery that we created at Pallant House Gallery as a collaborative positive outcome from the Covid-19 pandemic. Maggi painted a 'naked night'. That miniature work packs a punch despite its

Maggi Hambling.
Photograph by Douglas Atfield.

diminutive size. I hope that in time we can represent Maggi in our permanent collection with a larger work befitting her place in the history of British art. For now, I am delighted that we are showing her latest body of paintings for the first time.

Last year, Maggi and I were sat next each to each other in Sally Clarke's restaurant at a dinner for the Artists' Collecting Society, of which we are both Trustees. When I asked her what she had been working on recently, she told me about a new series of paintings inspired by hearing nightingales sing in the Sussex woodland. With wry humour she described sinking into the mud, but also, touchingly, how she had been struck by the beauty of what she heard. I must confess that it didn't immediately strike me as a likely subject for her work, but since I run a museum of modern art in Sussex, my interest was naturally piqued. On seeing the resulting paintings in Maggi's studio, our Chief Curator Melanie Vandenbrouck and I were both entranced by their lyricism and the way in which they evoke the intangible quality of birdsong through golden hues of paint. We were also amused to hear birdsong in her London studio, courtesy of an RSPB clock, every hour, on the hour.

Inspired by Maggi's paintings, this spring Melanie and I each spent an evening in the Sussex woodland with the folksinger Sam Lee experiencing the nightingales sing in an aural to-and-fro with Sam and other singers. It was a magical experience, but also intensely poignant as these birds are now on the red list of endangered species. Maggi's paintings thus capture the fleeting and ephemeral quality of this experience, but also record something that is at risk due to the impact of global warming and species extinction.

Maggi is part of an illustrious roster of writers and artists who have responded to nightingale song, from John Keats' 'Ode to a Nightingale' to the various vocalists from Vera Lynn and Frank Sinatra to Nat King Cole and Twiggy who have sung 'A Nightingale Sang in Berkeley Square'. Alongside her paintings inspired by nightingale song we also present works inspired by the songs of Leonard Cohen, PJ Harvey, Nick Cave and Will Young. Each is testament to how Maggi is inspired by one form

Maggi Hambling's London studio, 2024.
Photograph by Simon Martin.

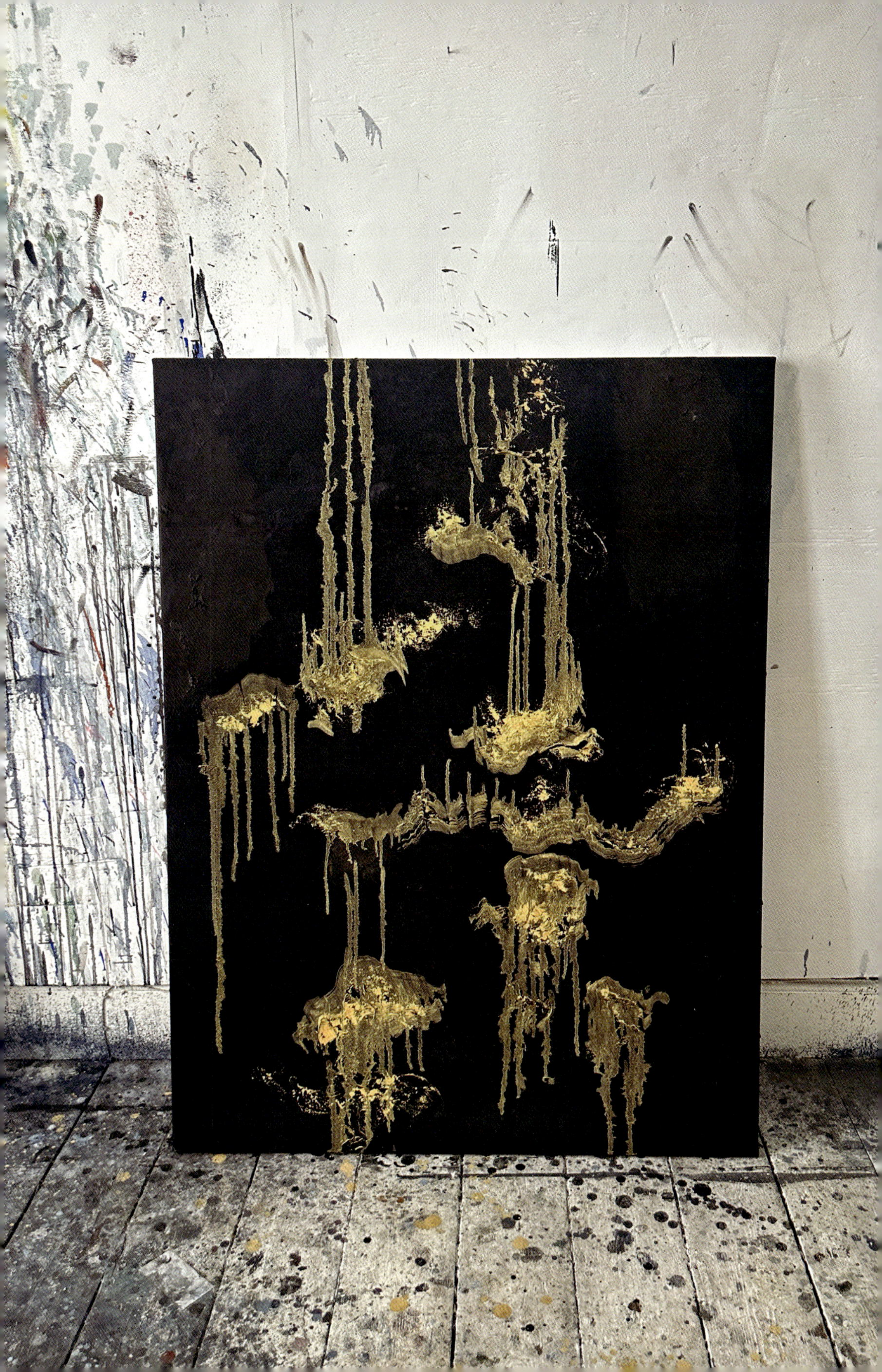

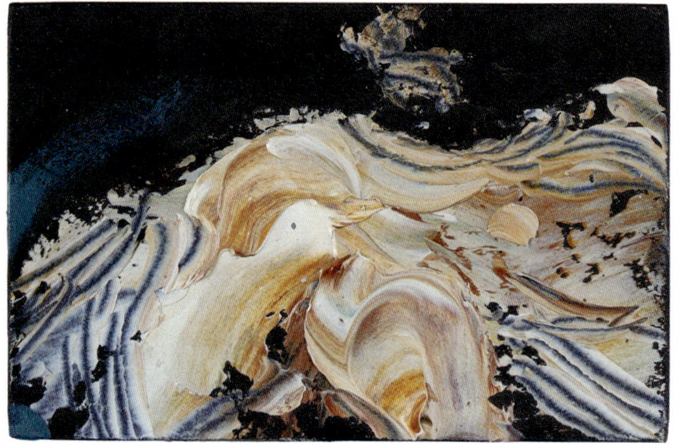

Naked Night, 2020
From 'The 2021 Model Art Gallery'
Oil on board, 9.5 x 14.2 cm
Pallant House Gallery, Chichester
Presented by the artist, 2020.

of artistry – song – to create another in paint. Will Young has
described it thus:

> *Having your portrait painted is an experience. Having your
> portrait painted by your friend and neighbour who is Maggi
> Hambling is quite another. 'You've moved again William...
> will you please stop F**KING moving!' It's hard to not talk
> and also giggle when around Maggi. There is of course the
> 'stare' – Maggi stares at you, daring you to be, well... to be
> yourself. She looks into you and brings out something I didn't
> even know was in there (or perhaps I did, I've had enough
> therapy). She pulls out the song, the melancholy, the melody,
> the existential angst, the desperation to be noticed and the
> plea that I matter to the world. And this is the defining thing
> with Maggi: you do matter, she cares and she sees you.*

Will Young's comments capture something important about
Maggi: the sense of care. Just as Gilbert White, the 18th-century
naturalist, taught us when he wrote about the nightingale: in
order to care for something, you have to first notice it; to give it
time and attention. In her latest series of works Maggi inspires us
to pause and consider the beauty of something fleeting laid down
in paint.

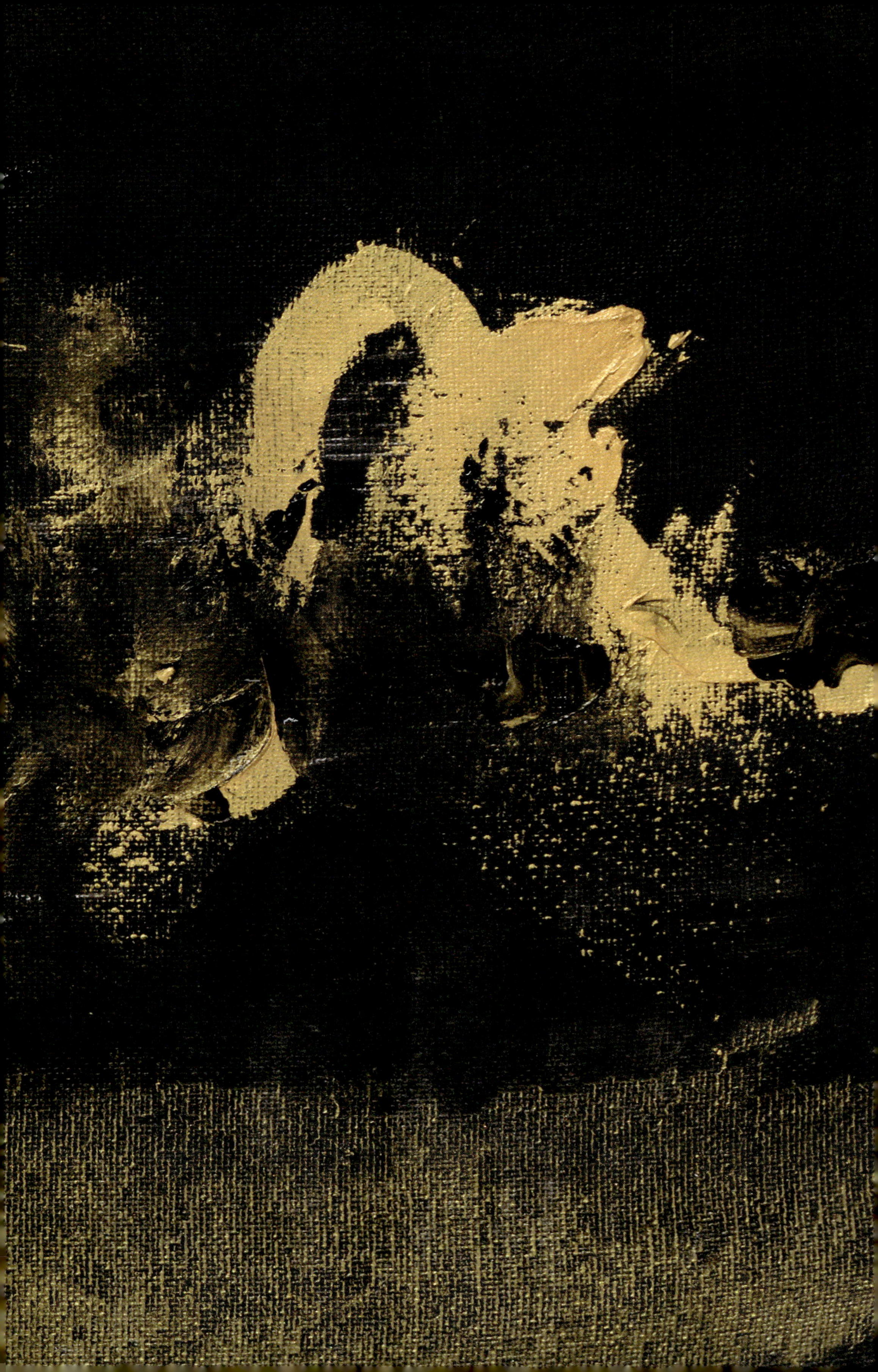

A Savage Kind of Brilliance

Maggi Hambling's *Nightingale night*

James Cahill

The cradle rocks above an abyss, and the common sense tells us that our existence is but a brief crack of light between two eternities of darkness.
Vladimir Nabokov, *Speak, Memory: An Autobiography Revisited* (1951)

Last spring in the woodlands of Sussex, Maggi Hambling experienced an unlikely epiphany. As part of a great friend's birthday celebrations, she and other guests ventured through the forest to a place where nightingales sing by night. In the darkness and pouring rain, folk musician Sam Lee and a fellow performer accompanied the birds by voice and violin. The rest of the party sat around on stools. The hour or so that Hambling spent listening to the birds gave rise to a new group of paintings titled *Nightingale night* (2023–24). A set of variations in gold paint on black, these recapture the strangeness and wonder of that brief interval of time, evoking the calls of the birds as scatterings and rivulets of iridescence.

'I felt touched by the sublime', Hambling recalls.[1] 'I always remember a tiny print by Hokusai of people contemplating Mount Fuji – we've lost that sense of awe at the contemplation of bigger things.' And yet her paintings, for all their sense of the epic, are records of the small-scale and the contingent, down to the vagaries of their own medium – flecks and drips and dissolving hazes. In this regard, too, the works are an apt reflection of that night in Sussex. As she listened to the birdsong, Hambling's stool and those of the other guests began to sink into the mud. The incongruity of the moment provoked laughter, but perhaps also carried a sense of the inevitable (as if nothing could be *purely*

[1] This and subsequent quotes from an interview with the artist, 29 May 2024.

Nightingale night V, 2023 (detail)
Oil on canvas, 59.7 x 40.6 cm

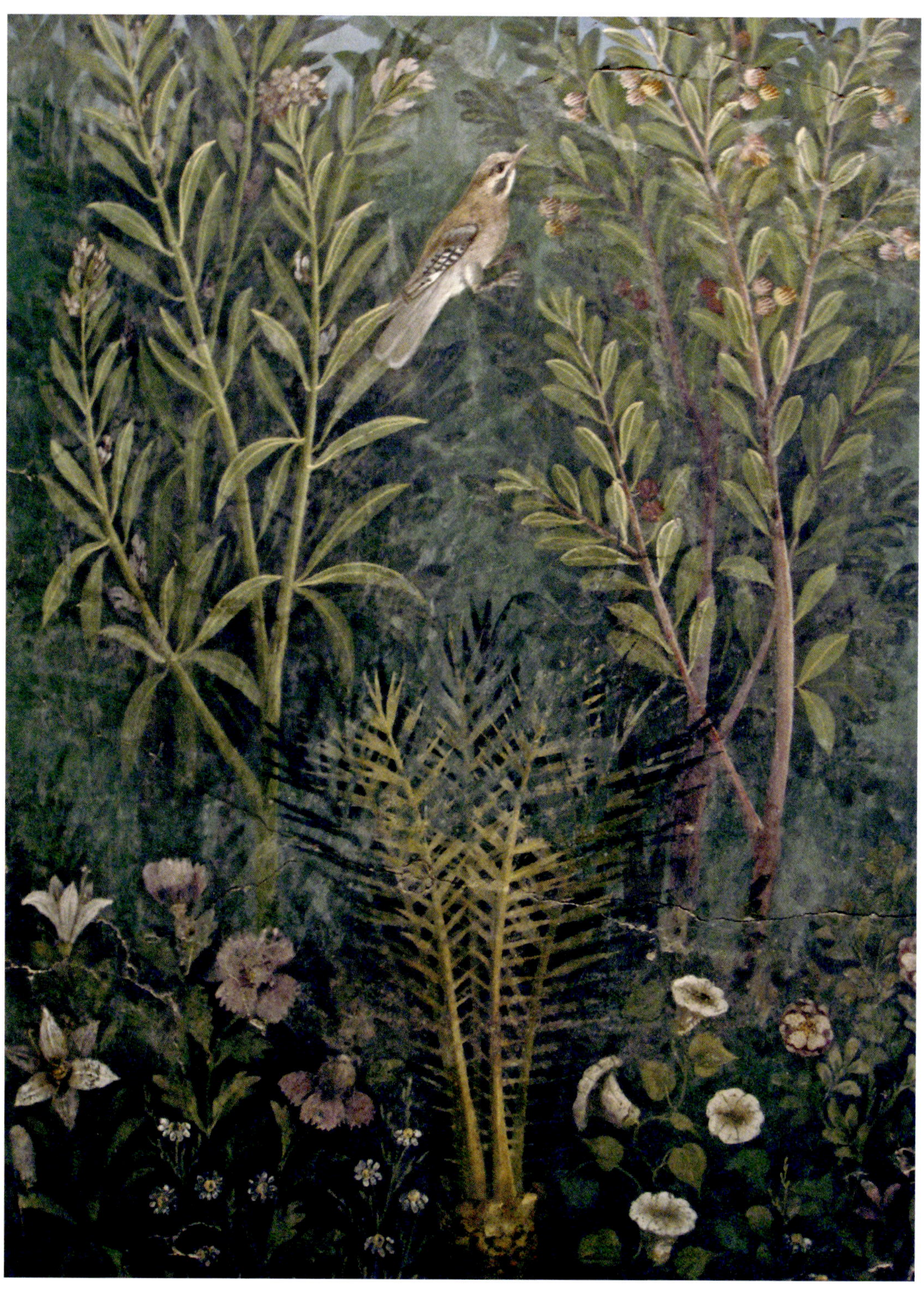

2 W.H. Auden, 'If I Could Tell You', 1940, first printed as 'Villanelle', *Vice-Versa*, January–February 1941. Hambling's incongruous experience – the soaring birdsong, the sinking into mud – also carries a faint echo of Oscar Wilde's line (in *Lady Windermere's Fan*, 1892): 'We are all in the gutter, but some of us are looking at the stars'. The statement is engraved on Hambling's 1998 sculpture of Wilde rising from his coffin, *A Conversation with Oscar Wilde*, situated outside Charing Cross Station, London.

Fresco of oleander and strawberry tree (detail), Julio-Claudian Era (35–45 CE), House of the Golden Bracelet, Pompeii, wall painting no.32. © Stefano Bolognini.

sublime), striking the same note of fatalism that we find in W.H. Auden's lines: 'If we should stumble when musicians play, / Time will say nothing but I told you so'.[2]

For all their celestial overtones, Hambling's latest paintings are reminders of ordinary, earthbound nature. Everywhere, the lustre of gold paint gives way to oozing physicality. No epiphany in her art (as in life) is absolute and whole. Such a doubling of the sublime and the commonplace is embodied in the nightingale itself, an unremarkable-looking brown bird from which a transcendental sound emerges. Since antiquity, the nightingale, whose name derives from Old English (a compound of the words for 'night' and 'sing'), has existed between mundane and mythic worlds. A living – endangered – species, it is also prolifically symbolic, an invention of tradition as much as of nature. The bird might be seen as a figure for Hambling's own apprehension of the natural world, whereby nature is visceral and untameable on the one hand, and on the other infused with metaphoric potential.

The *Nightingale night* series is a paean to nature in both these respects. Hambling has used gold paint – a pigment redolent of Byzantine and early Renaissance icons, in which it signified the divine, as well as Islamic and Asian traditions – to represent the epiphany of birdsong. The colour conveys a Biblical sense of revelation amid darkness, as well as a more pantheistic joy in nature. In its luminosity of theme and medium, the series stands in counterpoint to Hambling's *Maelstrom* paintings (2022–23) – disintegrations of flesh-tones and grey, in which the trauma of her recent heart attack blurred together with a response to the war in Ukraine. Her depictions of the nightingale's song appear, by contrast, to extol life and beauty. As with much of Hambling's art, however, an intimation of mortality lingers with the quiet insistence of the Latin inscription in Nicolas Poussin's *Et in Arcadia Ego* (1637–38; Musée du Louvre, Paris), where death asserts its presence in the midst of a pastoral idyll: 'I too am here in Arcadia'. Even as the gold colouration affirms life, blazing out from depthless black, it presages its own dissolution.

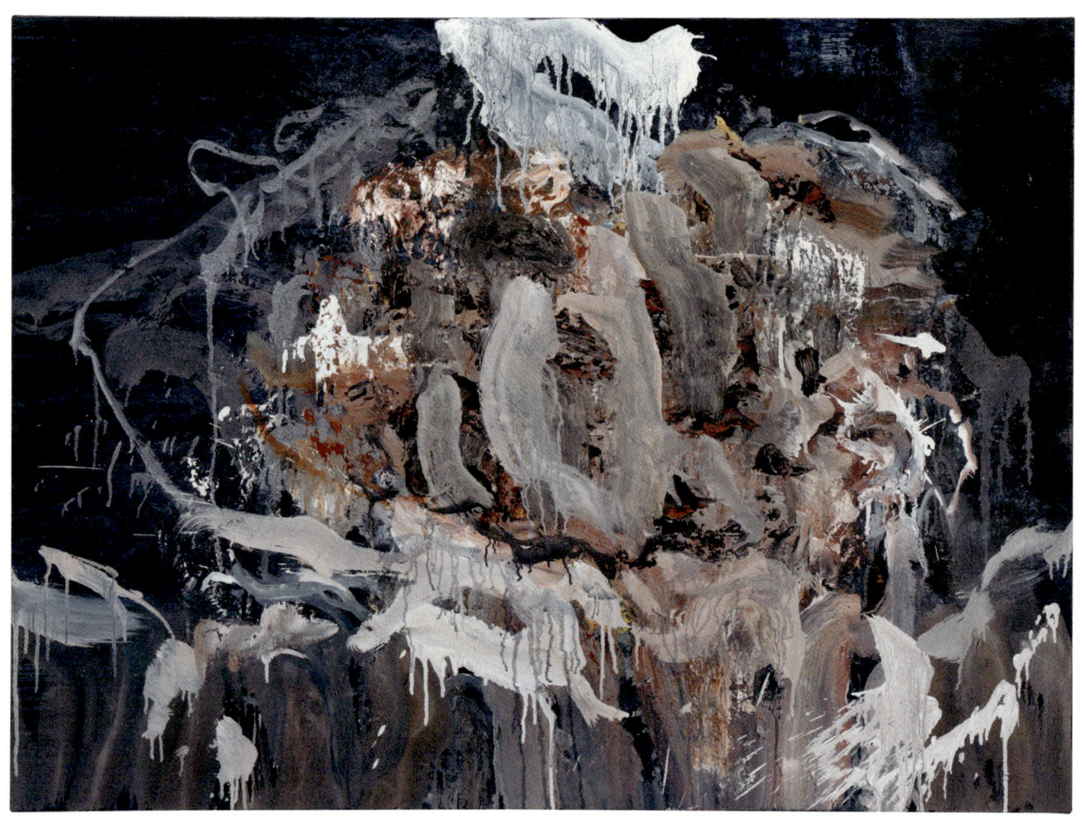

Maelstrom III, 2022
Oil on canvas, 91.4 x 121.9 cm
Photograph by Douglas Atfield

At Pallant House, the *Nightingale night* paintings form
the core of an exhibition dedicated to Hambling's depiction of
sound. At one level, the works reprise a theme that has recurred
in her art for more than a decade. For her 2012 installation *You
Are the Sea*, she combined a *Wall of Water* painting (one of a
series of depictions of exploding waves) with a soundtrack of
sluicing water and distorted voices. Her *War Requiem* paintings
of 2013 formed an accompaniment to Benjamin Britten's
1962 mass for the dead, with the two elements juxtaposed in
a single-room installation.[3] For *Relic* (2021), she collaborated
with sound artist Chris Watson on an installation of plaster
sculptures evoking Arctic wastes, set against the refracted noise
of disintegrating ice.

More recently, the idea of song transmitted through paint
– the visual representation of sound – has become a dominant
concern. Gold paint has taken on a new prominence. *Night
of the Lotus Eaters* (2019) was made as a response to the
eponymous song of 2008 by Nick Cave, whose lyrics invoke the
ancient story of an island where people feast on the lotus flower,
a plant that induces dreamy forgetfulness and a desire never to
leave ('Sapped and stupid / I lie upon the stones and I swoon').
Stuttering gold marks ascend the canvas in a diagonal formation,
trailing long rivulets. It is tempting to relate the hatchings and
drips – their flickering, plunging motions – not only to the
song's moody cadences, but to the myth behind the title: the
idea of an impossible place (whether physical or mental) where
blissful oblivion prevails, turning the past and future into
'identical twins' of darkness.[4]

The painting *Leonard Cohen* (2016–17) is an earlier
forerunner to the *Nightingale night* cycle. It employs the same
palette of gold on black to communicate the power of the
singer's voice, its persistence in the memory. 'I was trying to
paint the sound of Leonard Cohen for some weeks after he died',
Hambling recounts. 'And then quite suddenly that portrait
happened.' The brushstrokes cohere into the image of a head
silhouetted in negative against the black. And yet the subject
is more a sensation than a specific form. The clustering gold

3 *You Are the Sea*, 'SNAP: Art at the
Aldeburgh Festival', Snape Maltings,
Suffolk, 9–24 June 2012; *War Requiem
and Aftermath*, 'SNAP: Art at the
Aldeburgh Festival', Snape Maltings,
Suffolk, 8–30 June 2013; 'Relic:
Maggi Hambling & Chris Watson',
Snape Maltings, Suffolk, 2 June –
31 August 2021.

4 Vladimir Nabokov, *Speak, Memory:
An Autobiography Revisited*, Vintage
Books, New York, 1989 (originally
published 1951), p.19.

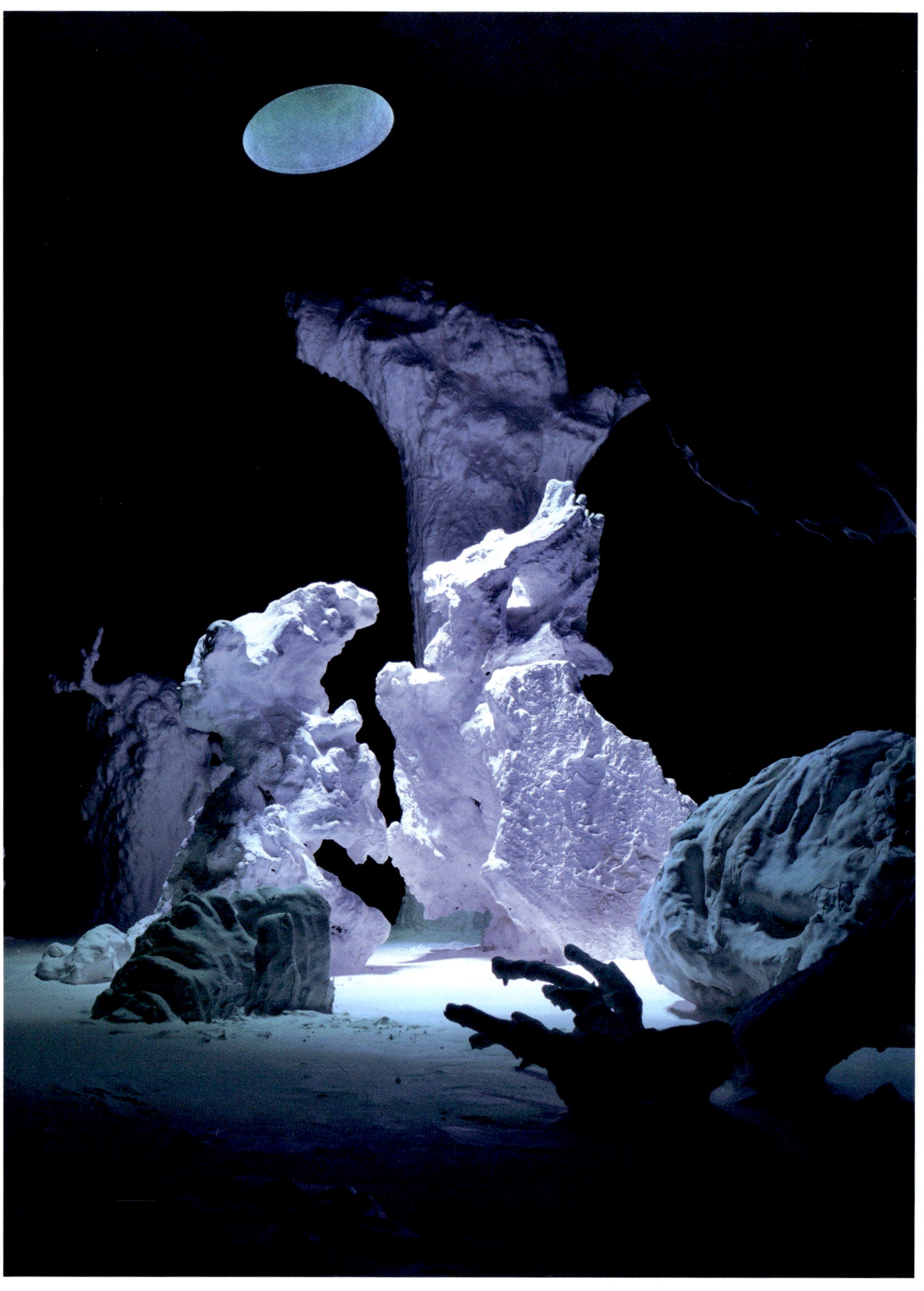

marks, subtended by thread-like drips, express the fluctuating resonance of Cohen's voice, the poetry of his lyrics, the inconstancy of his song. (In a line from 'Tower of Song' [1988], Cohen confessed: 'I was born like this, I had no choice / I was born with the gift of a golden voice'.) In a foreshadowing of the *Nightingale night* series, the intimacy of the painting contains within it the semblance of a cosmic event, something gigantic and primordial. This too expresses a fundamental aspect of Cohen's music. As Bob Dylan remarked shortly before Cohen's death: 'His melodies ... along with his lyrics, are his greatest genius ... Even the counterpoint lines – they give a celestial character and melodic lift to his songs'.[5]

A silhouetted head reappears in two self-portraits, *Listening to nightingales* (both 2023), in which Hambling depicts herself in pulsing gold marks. These cohere into human shape while equally conveying the dissolution of the self – the loss of self-awareness that an epiphany might induce. The head appears atomised and airborne, like that portrayed by Salvador Dalí in *Tête Raphaëlesque éclatée [Exploding Raphaelesque Head]* (1951; Scottish National Gallery, Edinburgh), or like any of the impasto heads that Hambling has painted since her *Victims* series of 2012 (part of *War Requiem*), in which colliding colours take the place of recognisable features.

Like the two portraits, the *Nightingale night* paintings are images of transition. They speak variously of the merging of environment and self, the transformation of a bird's call into 'song' (nature resolving into art) and the translation of music into painting. Each thereby expresses a kind of synaesthesia, embodying one medium through another. At the same time, they express the incapacities of each medium, hinting at what *cannot* be vocalised or visualised. In this, there is an echo of the Renaissance practice of *paragone*, whereby the merits of two different art forms (painting and sculpture, art and poetry) were serially debated. The curtains or grilles of drips that descend across each canvas underscore the general sense of unresolved transition, reminding us of the fluidity of the medium itself – its capacity to bleed from form into trickling

[5] Bob Dylan, quoted in David Remnick, 'Leonard Cohen Makes It Darker', *The New Yorker*, 10 October 2016.

Relic, 2021
Maggi Hambling and Chris WatsonMultimedia sculpture and sound installation. Photograph by Douglas Atfield.

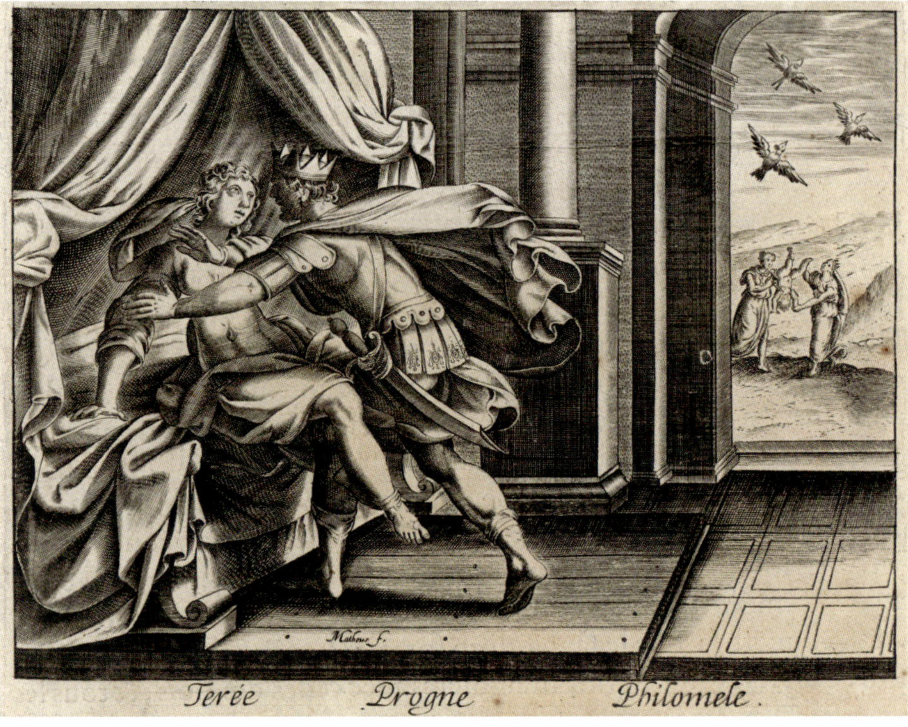

formlessness. What might be filigree threads are streaming, untransformed paint.

The nightingale symbolises these various kinds of transformation. The Roman poet Ovid, in his *Metamorphoses* (c.8 CE), tells the story of Philomel and Procne, a myth that not only invests the nightingale with symbolic resonance but collapses together several of the transformations implied by Hambling's paintings: between beauty and abjection, sound and silence, or life's ephemerality and art's immortalising power. Tereus, King of Thrace, married Procne, daughter of the King of Athens. A child, Itys, was born amid great celebration. Five years later, Procne requested to be allowed to see her sister, Philomel. Tereus sailed to Athens, and having set eyes on the young girl, was consumed by lust. He contrived to take her back to Thrace, where he raped her and, to ensure her silence, cut out her tongue. Philomel wove an account of the crime in a tapestry ('wrote purple signs into white threads', as Ovid relates) and thus revealed her fate to her sister. Together, Philomel and Procne murdered the infant boy, Itys, and fed him to Tereus. Realising what he had done,

Jean Matheus (1590–1672), *Terée, Procne, Philomele*, engraving, illustration for Nicolas Renouard's French translation of Ovid's *Metamorphoses*, Paris, veuve Langelier, 1619. © Chronicle / Alamy Stock Photo.

6 Ovid, *Metamorphoses*, 6.412–674.
   In Greek, 'Philomel' – literally 'lover
   of song' – comes to mean 'nightingale'.
   In other sources, for example the
   Bibliotheca of Pseudo-Apollodorus,
   Procne is the nightingale and
   Philomel (or Philomela) the swallow.

the king flew at the sisters with his sword, and the three of them were transformed: Philomel into a nightingale, Procne into a swallow, Tereus into an aggressive hoopoe.[6]

It is a lurid, winding story. The connection with Hambling's gold paintings might seem oblique, and yet the ancient myth offers a lens through which to examine the layered effects of her art. Beneath the violent theatricality of Ovid's account is a theme of endurance in both senses of the word: the victim's survival of her ordeal and the perpetuation of her voice, first in the form of a work of art (the tapestry that substitutes for spoken words) and finally in a fact of nature – the nightingale's song. In the broadest sense, Hambling's art rests upon the idea that any experience – whether of pain or pleasure or desire – might be subsumed, or translated, into an image or an object. Each of her paintings, she has often said, is an act of remembrance. She writes 'signs' of her experience, as Philomel did, in her works, and in this way her art betokens both loss and survival, like the nightingale's song.

Listening to nightingales I contains within modest proportions its own ranging sense of metamorphosis – of corporeal form dissolving into something airborne and uncatchable, and yet enduring (as the sideways-streaming drips imply) like sound carried on the air. At the centre of the picture, a silver-grey 'nucleus', in which we might discern a fragment of a human figure, recedes behind a nebula of gold flickers. In *Nightingale night V*, the flung paint could almost represent the swooping and flapping of birds. By contrast, there is a restrained poise about the gold marks in *Nightingale night II*, which punctuate the black ground like embroidered motifs – stray crests or curlicues, offcuts of Baroque décor. But still the threat of formlessness lingers: the trickling rivulets seem to presage an unravelling, as if threads had begun to be unpicked. The 'signs' that Hambling has woven into her composition are in this way equivocal – tokens of *undoing*. Even as they blaze out like gilt calligraphy, they connote a loss of legibility, a breaking down of order.

The transmutations of the ancient myth find a counterpart, then, in Hambling's mercurial paintwork – its shifts from ornamentality to base materialism and back again. Equally, the paintings channel the idea of a song that has endured in defiance of time and history. T.S. Eliot, in a passing reference to the Philomel myth in 'The Waste Land' (1922), refers to the nightingale that 'filled all the desert with inviolable voice'. Suspended against a 'desert' of dense black, Hambling's gathering or dispersing gold paintwork has about it the same air of inviolability, a savage kind of brilliance. Paradoxically, it seems all the more inviolable for its underlying note of fragility, its hint of imminent decay. The implied movement of the paint is always ambiguous, poised between falling apart and falling together. As Eliot goes on to say, the nightingale's song is a mere 'Jug jug to dirty ears': beauty can shade in an instant into dull ordinariness. It is characteristic of Hambling's art that the paintings' mythic resonances dissolve before one's eyes into the 'dirt' of hurled, smeared and dripping paint.

The nightingale's song equally is an elegy, a *miserabile carmen* according to Virgil in the *Georgics* (29 BCE), or as Edith Sitwell wrote in her 1927 poem 'The Little Ghost Who Died for Love', 'it is the cold sends quivering / My voice, a little nightingale that grieves. / Now Time beats not, and dead Love is forgotten'.[7] In this instance, the call of the nightingale is akin to the voice of a ghost, a spirit that strives to expel memories of love and the 'lost world': the imagery of the poem wavers between vivid recollections of that world and expressions of dark oblivion ('It is so cold now that my heart is dead / And drops through time … night is too dark to see').[8] In the case of Philomel, suffering has been consigned to the call of a bird, sustained but also effaced; after all, the nightingale's 'lament' is really a mating call. Likewise, Hambling's paintings are both exuberant and elegiac: gold paint waltzes across the void and yet the blackness seems to swallow the light. Just as the mythic story fails to resolve, its human conflict transmuting into a spectacle of birds in flight, her paintings refuse to condense into a finite image or to settle into a single emotional key.

Another more recent parallel to Hambling's series is Andy Warhol's group of *Oxidation* or 'Piss' paintings of 1977–78.[9] In these, a basic function of the body gives rise to shimmering,

[7] The imagined speaker of Edith Sitwell's poem is a latter-day Philomel, the ghost of a 17th-century woman who was unjustly hanged, singing a lament after death.

[8] See Jane Dowson and Alice Entwistle, *A History of Twentieth-Century British Women's Poetry*, Cambridge University Press, Cambridge, 2005, pp.64–5.

[9] I am grateful to Dr Donato Esposito for pointing out this connection.

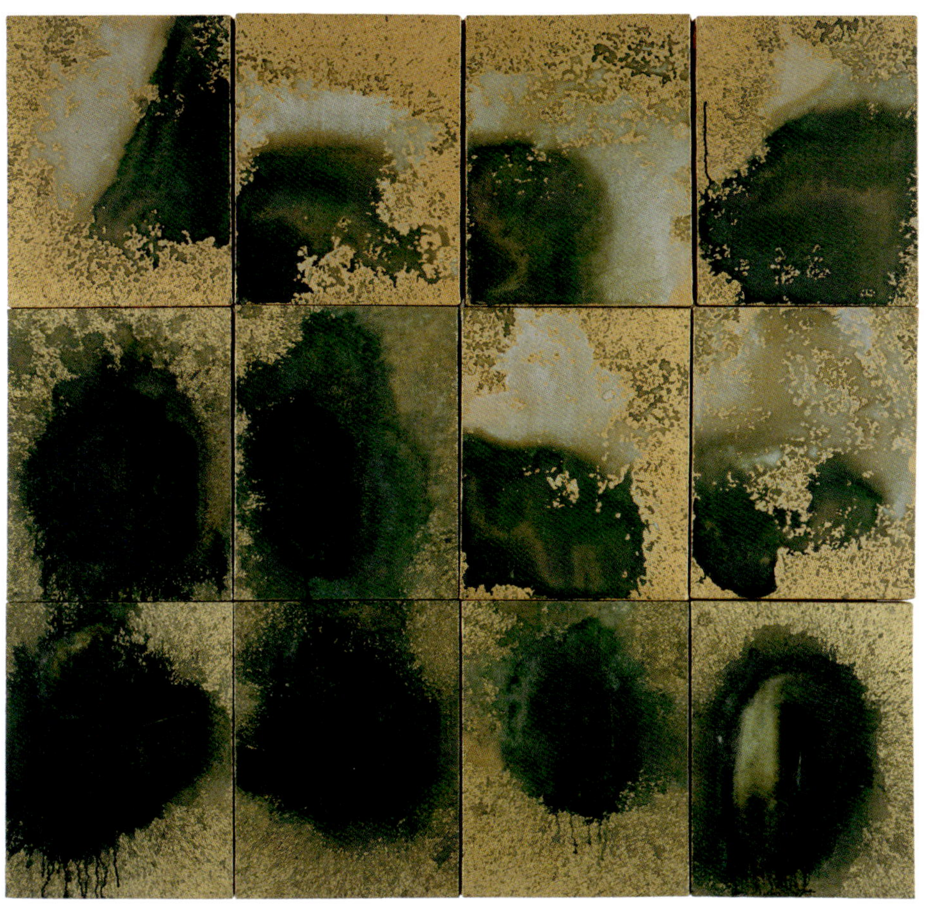

Andy Warhol (1928–1987),
Oxidation Painting (in 12 parts),
1978, 121.9 x 124.5 cm. The Andy
Warhol Museum, Pittsburgh.
© 2024 The Andy Warhol
Foundation for the Visual Arts, Inc. /
Licensed by DACS, London.

variegated abstractions. Warhol created the paintings by urinating (or having assistants urinate) onto copper-coated canvases; the uric acid oxidised the metal to create a discoloured surface in which the metallic sheen disperses amid outbreaks of green and black. These works enact a sort of alchemical transformation of bodily waste into aesthetic form, and yet that transformation is not clear-cut: the final paintings retain a degraded quality (dripping, spattered, stained) while the original act of urination had an aspect of artistic purpose to it. As Warhol observed: 'If I asked someone to do an *Oxidation* painting, and they just wouldn't think about it, it would be a mess ... you try to figure out a good design'.[10] Warhol's series – a subversive, self-reflexive take on Jackson Pollock's method of working 'flat' – closely prefigures the contradictions of Hambling's *Nightingale night* paintings, in which the poetry of the nightingale's song and the blunt force of 'Jug jug' co-exist in the very mutations of the paintwork. Like Warhol's, her paintings allude to, and gently subvert, the gestural abstraction of the mid-20th century, repeating at a more intimate scale the epic topographies of

Clyfford Still (1904–1980), *PH-48 (1957-D-No. 1)*, 1957, oil on canvas, 287 x 403.9 cm. Collection Buffalo AKG Art Museum, Buffalo, New York. © City & County of Denver, Courtesy Clyfford Still Museum / DACS 2024 / Buffalo AKG Art Museum / Art Resource, NY / Scala, Florence.

[10] Benjamin H.D. Buchloh, 'An Interview with Andy Warhol', 1985, reproduced in ed. Kenneth Goldsmith, *I'll Be Your Mirror: The Selected Andy Warhol Interviews, 1962–1987*, Carroll & Graf, New York, 2004, pp.321–32, p.327.

Clyfford Still (*Nightingale night III*) or the lyrical 'soak stains' of Helen Frankenthaler (*Nightingale night VII*).

Warhol, whose embrace of mass culture belied a fascination with religious iconography, has been a touchstone for Hambling since she came across his silkscreen work *Suicide (Fallen Body)* (1962) on a trip to Cologne in the late 1990s. This consists of the repeating image of a woman's body – a young suicide victim, photographed in 1947 after she jumped from the Empire State Building – on top of the crushed roof of a car. The woman's face has an expression of preternatural calm, or what Emily Brontë called an 'untroubled image of Divine rest'.[11] 'I stood looking at the picture for a long while', Hambling recalls, 'and I felt as if I were there while the woman was jumping off the building. That's what convinced me about Warhol being an artist.'

Like Warhol's *Oxidation* series, Hambling's paintings are records of their own making – testaments to a live act. The apparently abstract scheme in *PJ Harvey in concert* (2024) – a turmoil of grey, black, gold and crimson – conceals multiple images of the musician singing. More crucially, the painting is a re-enactment of the experience of hearing Harvey live, in the immersive setting of a concert. 'There she is, and there she is, and there she is', Hambling has said of the painting, 'and all the rest is sound.' The picture is a record of sensations, rather than a portrait in any conventional sense. In *Will Young* (2023), the subject materialises into clearer view, and yet the portrait is again an evocation of the liveness, the nowness, of the singer's presence. Young and his 'aura' are one and the same. The idea is made explicit by the diptych format: the human figure occupies one half, while a shower of gold erupts from his heart in the other, flaring out into darkness. It is a metaphor, perhaps, for his interiority – the projection of the inner being into the world.

'When you look at an oil painting', Hambling says, 'you feel – if it's any good – that it's being made in front of you, or you're part of the making. You enter into the whole thing yourself.' In asserting the 'live' quality of an oil painting, she has often pointed to the example of Rembrandt. The *Nightingale night* series invokes the diffuse, granular goldenness of

[11] Emily Brontë, *Wuthering Heights,* Penguin Books, London, 1995 (originally published 1847), p.169.

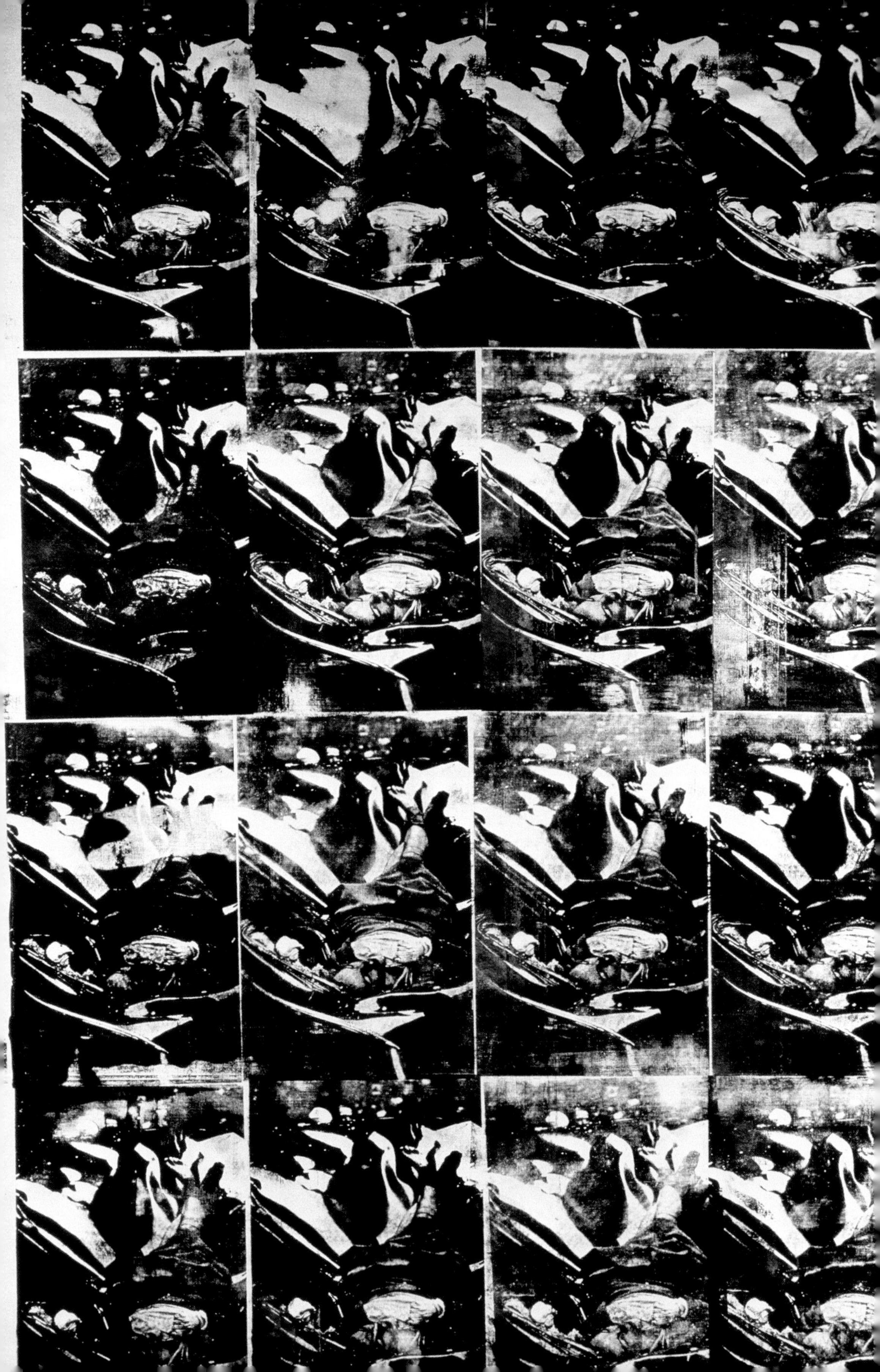

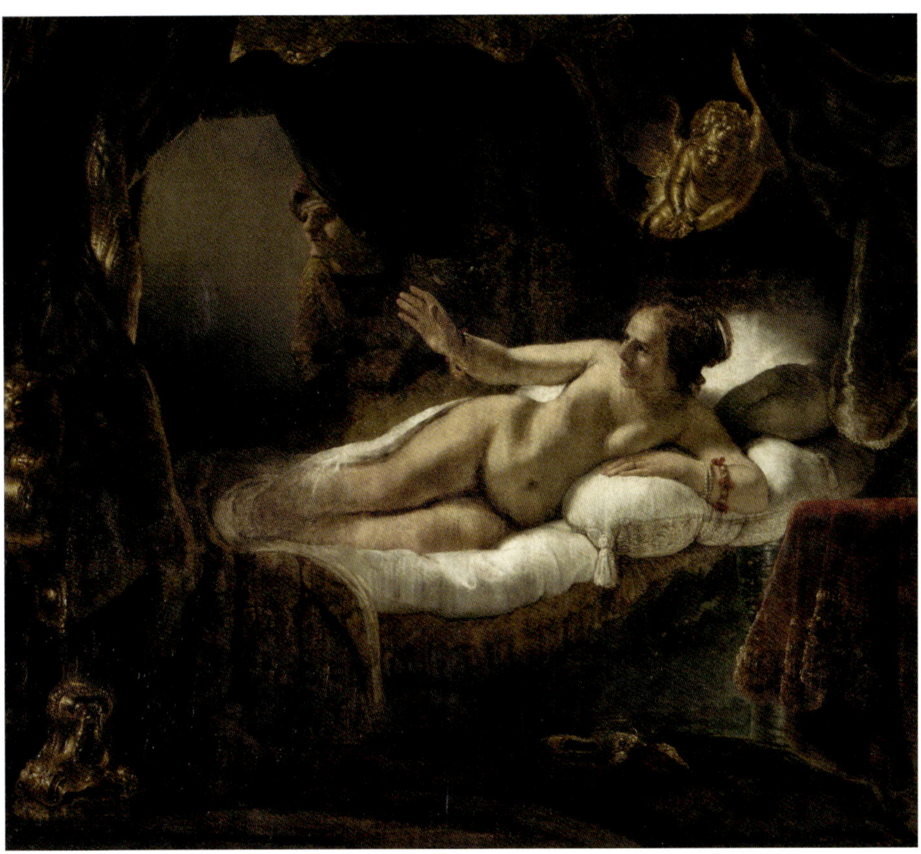

ABOVE Rembrandt van Rijn (1606–1669), *Danaë*, 1636–43, oil on canvas, 185 x 202.5 cm. © The State Hermitage Museum / Photo by Vladimir Terebenin.

OPPOSITE Andy Warhol (1928–1987), *Suicide (Fallen Body)*, 1962, silkscreen ink, silver paint on canvas, 284.5 x 204.2 cm. Private collection. Courtesy Doris Ammann / Thomas Ammann Fine Art. © 2024 The Andy Warhol Foundation for the Visual Arts, Inc. / Licensed by DACS, London.

12 Titian, *Danaë* (1544–6), oil on canvas, 120 cm × 172 cm. National Museum of Capodimonte, Naples.

Rembrandt's pictures, a quality that characterises his later work in particular, but which also finds emblematic expression in his grand mythological scene, *Danaë* (1636–43; State Hermitage Museum, St Petersburg). According to the ancient story, Danaë was locked away by her father, Acrisius, King of Argos, to prevent the fulfilment of an oracle that she would bear a son who would kill Acrisius. Jupiter, king of the gods, came to her in the form of a shower of gold, stealing into her bedchamber and impregnating her. Unusually, Rembrandt depicts the metamorphosed god not as an iridescent cloud or as a rainfall of coins (as Titian did, for example, in his version of 1544–6), but in the form of spreading light.[12] (There is evidence that Rembrandt painted over a more conventional representation of the story, made in the mid-1630s, substituting the Baroque character of his earlier style with a more realist one.[13]) Light glances over every object and surface: the curtains around the bed, the tassels of the mattress, the gilded cupid above Danaë's bed (weeping with his wrists bound – a symbol of her enforced chastity). It pools over Danaë's naked body in a reminder of Jupiter's desirous intent. And yet the effect might simply be that of intense sunlight; we remain, ultimately, in the bedroom of a Dutch courtesan, with 'Danaë's' slippers lying discarded beside the bed. The painting's 'transfiguration of the commonplace' is equivocal – a momentary possibility.[14]

Rembrandt's depiction of a light that steals in every direction, scattering and concentrating as if possessed of its own capricious agency, finds an equivalent in Hambling's volatile paintwork. Her gold medium ranges between moments of hard intensity and broader swathes of particles or haze, as evidenced by *Nightingale night VI*, where the pervasive, quicksilver character of Rembrandt's light – the almost dreamlike sense of a light that moves of its own volition – translates into spectacle of coalescing and dispersing colour. The washes of gold that flood out of the thicker, impasto paintwork, seem to move in contrary directions (upward and downward at once) as if each were possessed of its own logic. At the same time, the suggestion in Rembrandt's picture that this is only, in the end, a fragment of real life – that the light is not really animate, that the woman is not a character from myth – holds up a mirror to the realist essence of Hambling's series. An episode of quixotic beauty can still be the occasion of sinking laughingly into mud.

Hambling's description of an oil painting's capacity to engulf the viewer ('you enter the whole thing yourself') might also be applied to the epiphany of her night amid the nightingales. As she absorbed the sounds around her, she became attuned solely to the present. 'I was in the moment, at that time, *listening*. Each of these paintings seized one of those moments. When you make a painting of it, you're fixing one moment in time.' The *Nightingale night* paintings are testaments not only to the beauty and persistence of song (in the individual mind, or in the collective memory of cultural

13 Analysis has shown that in the earlier iteration of the painting, Danaë was pulling back the curtain with her head raised and the elderly nurse was more prominent; see Erwin Panofksy, 'Eros Bound: Concerning the Genealogy of Rembrandt's *Danaë*', translated by P. Wortsman, ed. Gert Schiff, *German Essays on Art History: Winckelmann, Burckhardt, Panofsky, and Others*, Continuum, New York, 1988, pp.255–75.

14 The phrase is Arthur Danto's; see Danto, *The Transfiguration of the Commonplace: A Philosophy of Art*, Harvard University Press, Cambridge MA, 1981.

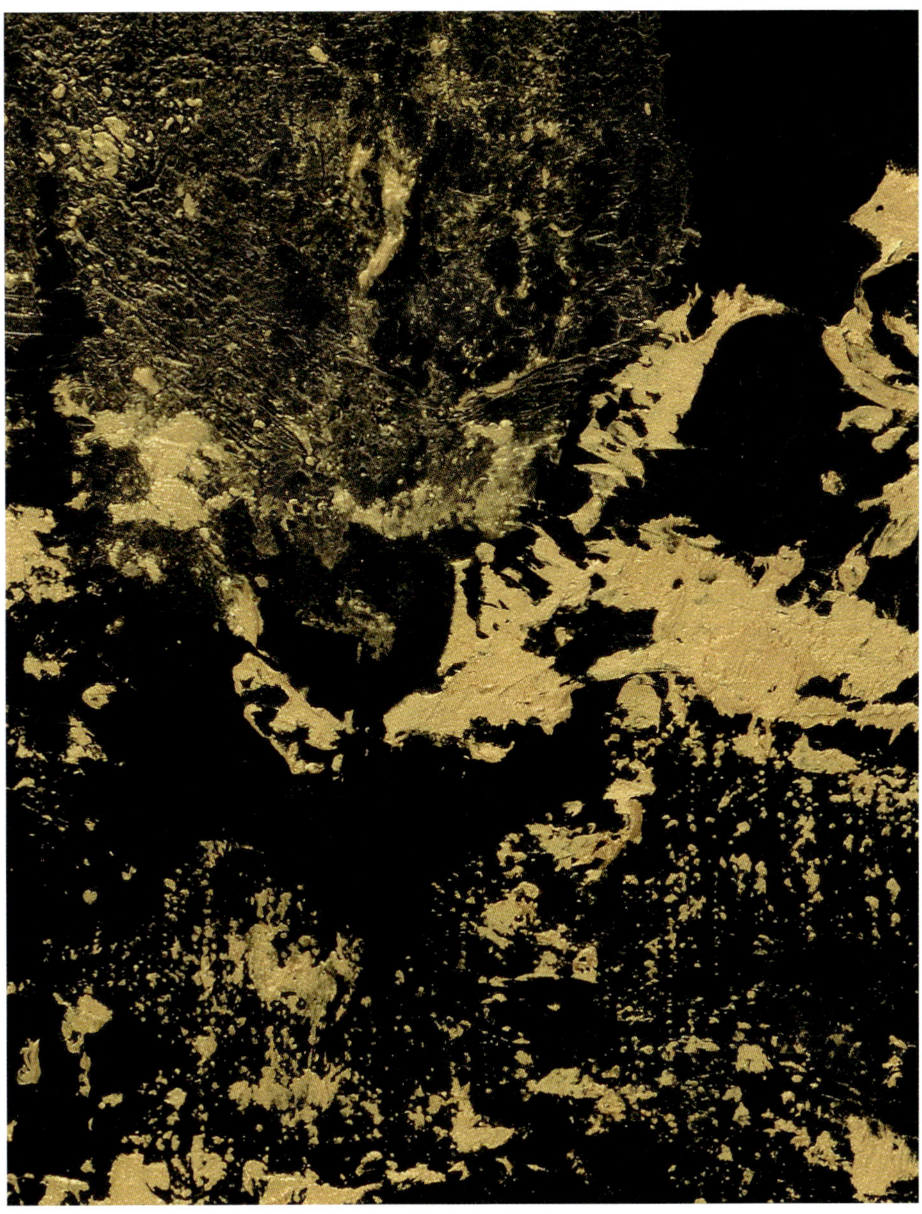

Nightingale night VI, 2023 (detail)
Oil on canvas, 53.3 x 43.2 cm

tradition), but to song's transience – its refusal to be fixed. More than anything, they transmit the double-edged nature of the nightingale's song, its combined joyfulness and lament. Their celebratory power is edged by a sense of loss. Death, as ever in Hambling's work, is life's counterpart – its defining 'other'; her flecks of gold signify embers as well as flames.

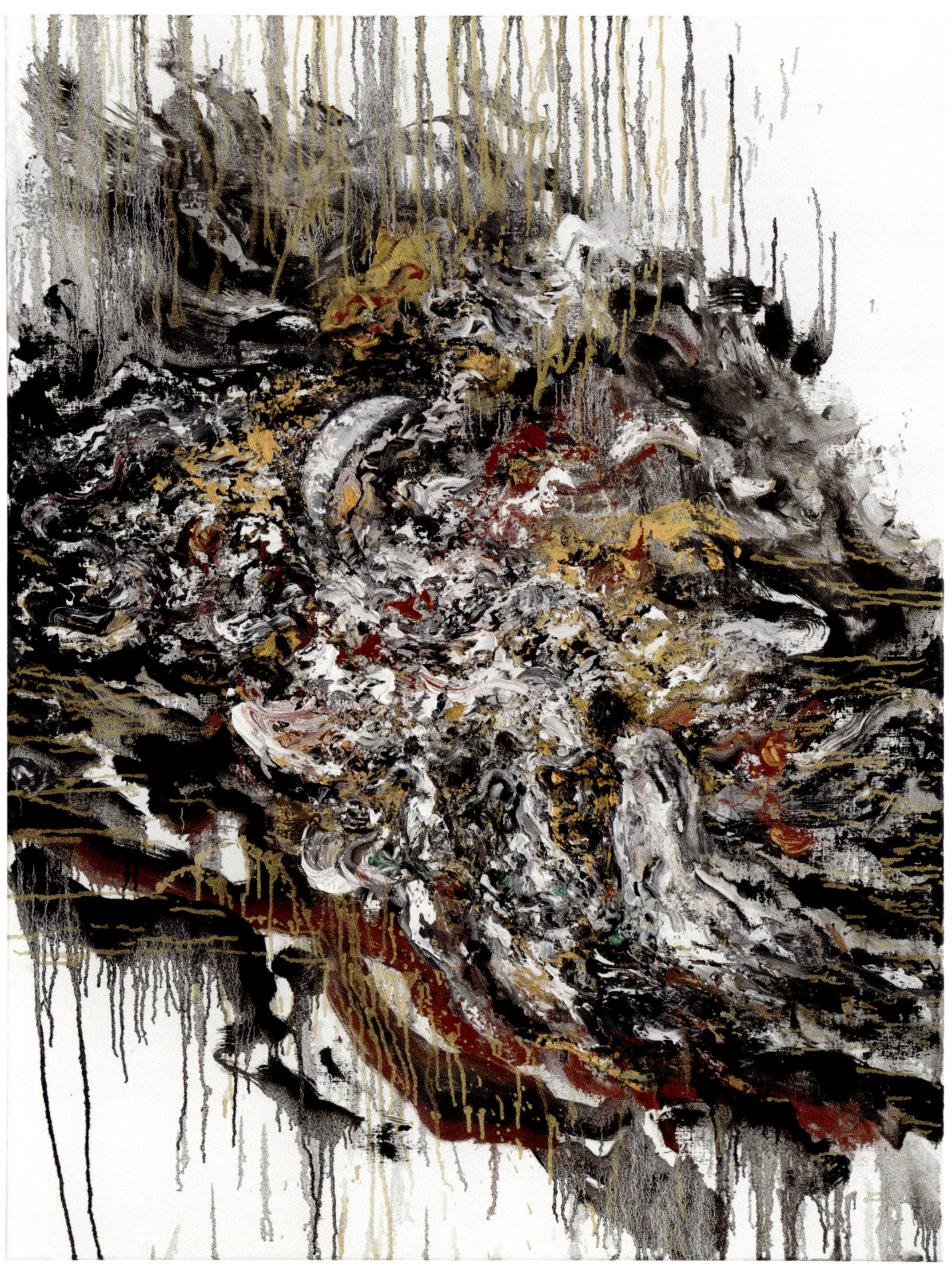

The Nightingale

PJ Harvey

I have heard the sound of your call
I have chosen your path
I joined your caravan
We called you 'The Nightingale'

I remember how excited we were
The best of life lay ahead for us
We marched on wrapped in your song
For you I gave my five-year-old son

I felt him behind me
I felt him helping me
Every one of us will go to paradise
He sang to the soldiers day and night
We called him 'The Nightingale'
Get ready, get ready, get ready

Heads on top of sticks were angels around me
Heads on top of sticks became angels around me
Heads on top of sticks, crushed veins, angels around me
Heads on top of sticks were like angels around me

PJ Harvey in Concert, 2023–24
Oil on canvas, 121.9 x 91.4 cm

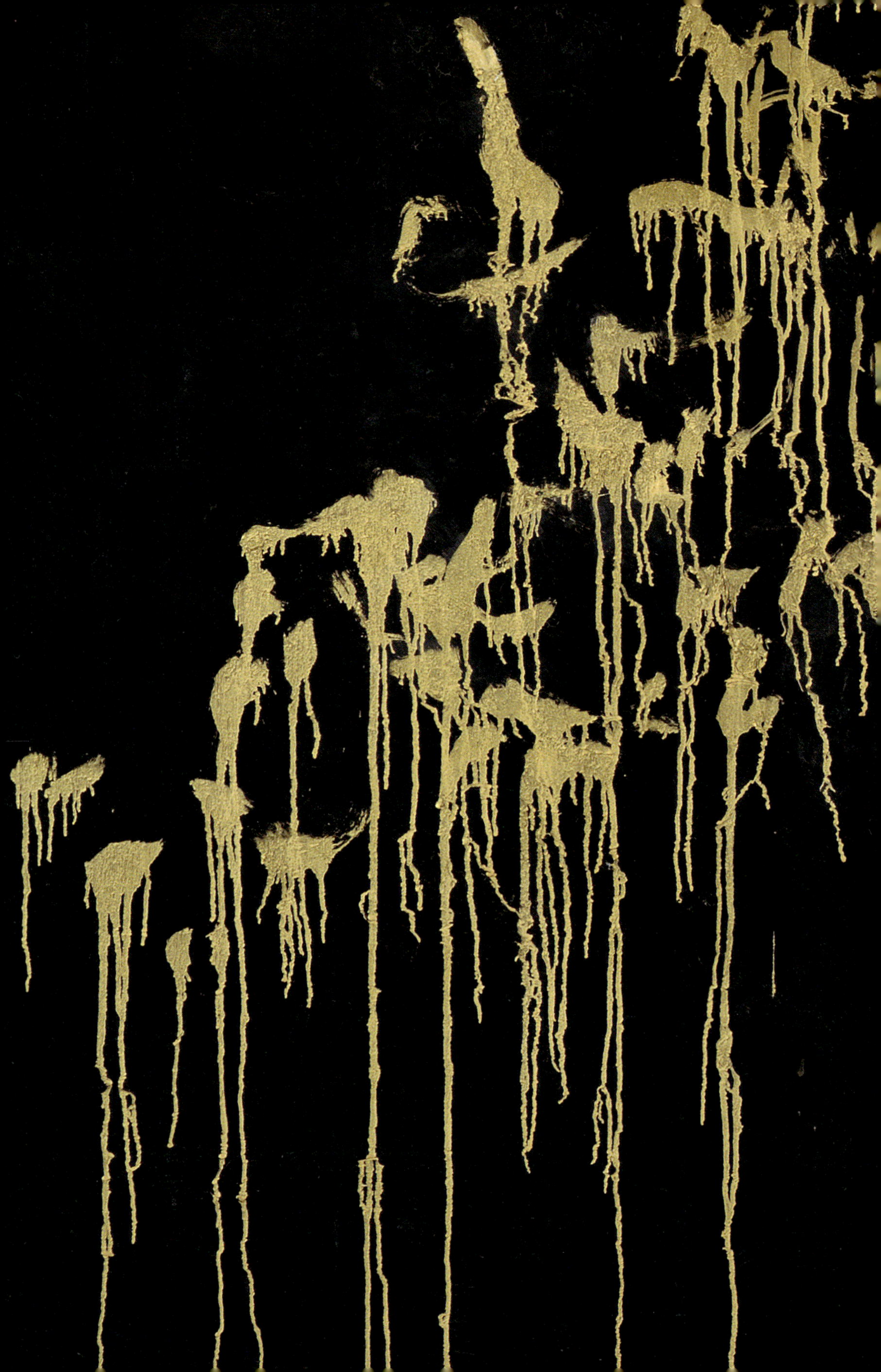

Night of the Lotus Eaters

Nick Cave

sapped & stupid

I lie upon the stones and I swoons

the darling little dandelions have done their thing

& changed from suns into moons

the dragons roam the shopping malls

I hear theyre gonna eat our guts

if I had the strength I might pick up my sword

& make some attempt to resist

get ready to shield yourself!!!!!!!!!

grab yr sap & yr heaters

get ready to shield yourself!!!!!!!!!

on the night of the lotus eaters

mmmmmmmm don't you love my baby

mmmmmmmm & don't you love my baby anymore

they gilded my scales / they fish-bowled me

& they toured me round the old aquariums

they come in their hordes to tap at the glass

the philistines and barbarians

I like

      floating

         here (it's nice)

theyve hung seaweed round my hips

& I do the

      <<hula>>

        for the hungry ones

Night of the Lotus Eaters, 2019 (detail)
Oil on canvas, 198.1 x 226.1 cm

Night of the Lotus Eaters, 2019 (detail)
Oil on canvas, 198.1 x 226.1 cm

& the lames all throw me tips

get ready to shield yourself!!!!!!!!!

grab yr sap & yr heaters

get ready to shield yourself!!!!!!!!!!

on the night of the lotus eaters

mmmmmmmm don't you love my baby

mmmmmmmm & don't you love my baby anymore

get ready to shield yourself!!!!!!!!!

from our catastrophic leaders

get ready to shield yourself!!!!!!!!!

grab yr sap & yr heaters

on the night of the lotus eaters

now hit the streets!!!!!!!

Now

    HIT

        the

         streets!!!!!!!!!!!!!!!!!!!!!!!!!!!!!!!

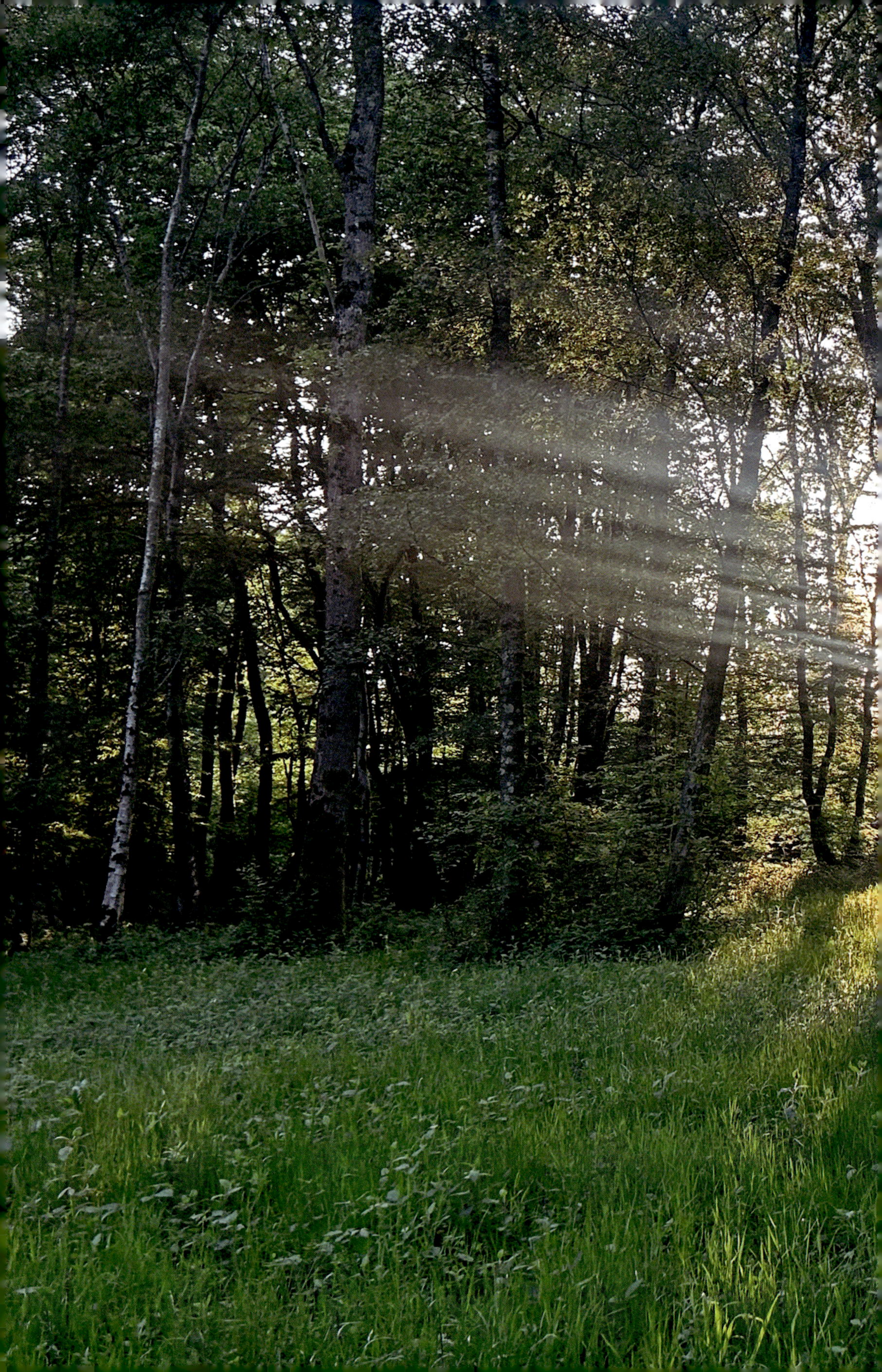

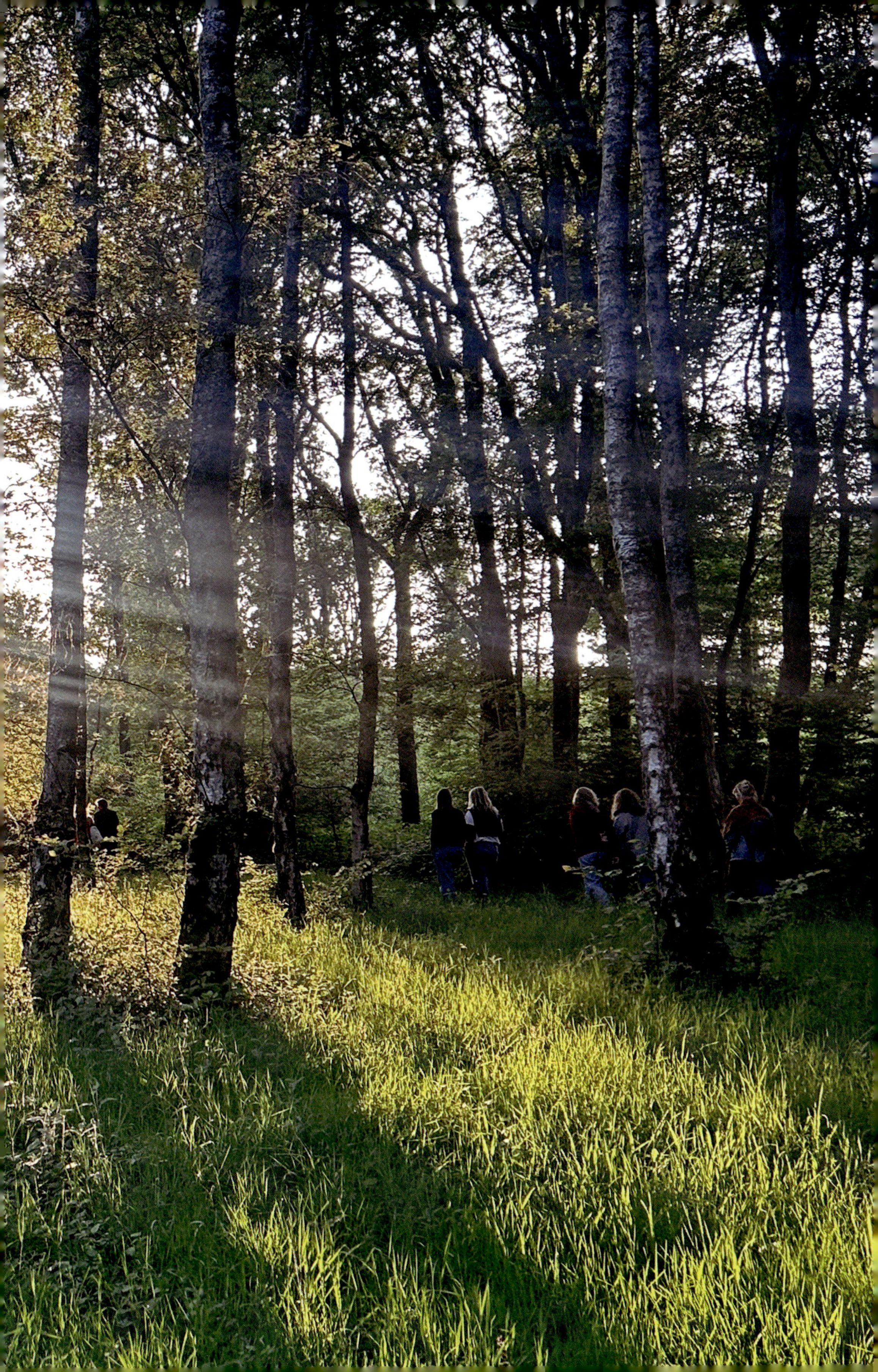

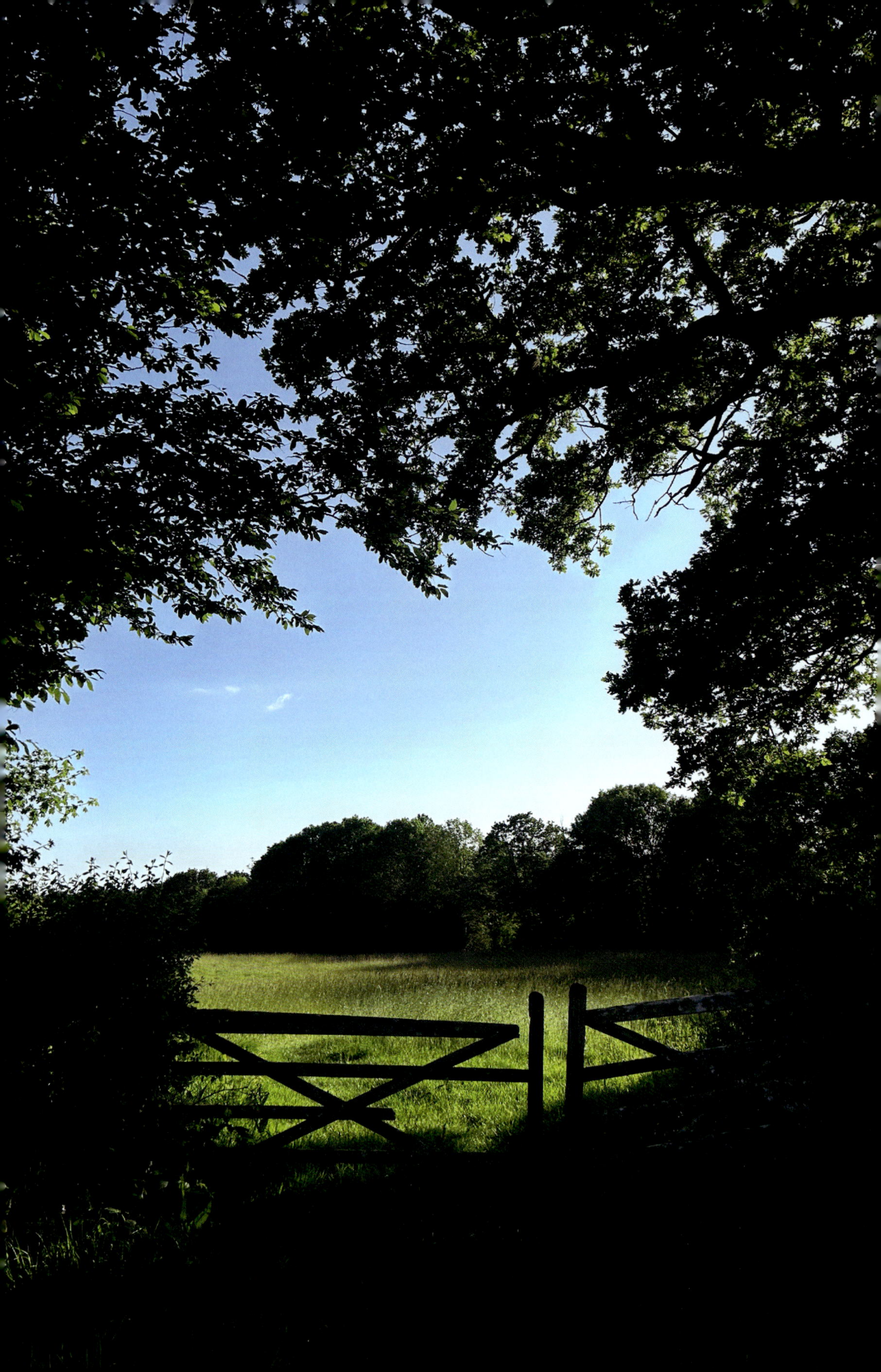

Decorations of Silence

Sam Lee

There is a long-held belief in folklore that while birds merely whistle, the nightingale *sings*. And what a concert this curious and elusive yet exuberant bird makes. These small, unassuming, brown-feathered, rufous-backed and light-chested warblers may not be much to look at but when darkness falls over our springtime, scrubby, coppiced landscapes, what infiltrates the crisp night air is a wonder of nature few species can rival. Their virtuosic, quixotic, ribald yet romantic, sinuous night-song ripples through a slumbering world, liquid and electric. It is a phenomenon, an evolutionary firework display, a decadence of soliloquies. For those who make the effort, a masterclass in prose, poise, projection and possession is received.

More than anything, this song is a harbinger of new life and bringer of hope. Nightingales summon. Those who have heeded the call recount the intoxication of a night spent in the close company of this mighty yet 'about-robin-sized' wonder bird. Their secretive yet voluminous song has acquired them, over the millennia, the status of muse or spirit guide to many of our great writers, artists and poets; inspiration for our scribes and a master of ceremonies to celebrators of land rites and keepers of the lore. But who is this bird, one known these days only vaguely through appearances in popular 'Mayfairous' melodies, stalking lovers in Berkeley Square, reduced nowadays to just a notion, a mere lyrical decorative gesture? How did this supercharged carrier of so much myth and motif end up culturally relegated to the shadows? Forgotten, bankrupt, evicted and existing as they do in life, literally skulking in the leaf litter, invisible and unrecognisable.

When the anthem 'A Nightingale Sang in Berkeley Square' was written in 1939, nightingales existed in the hundreds of

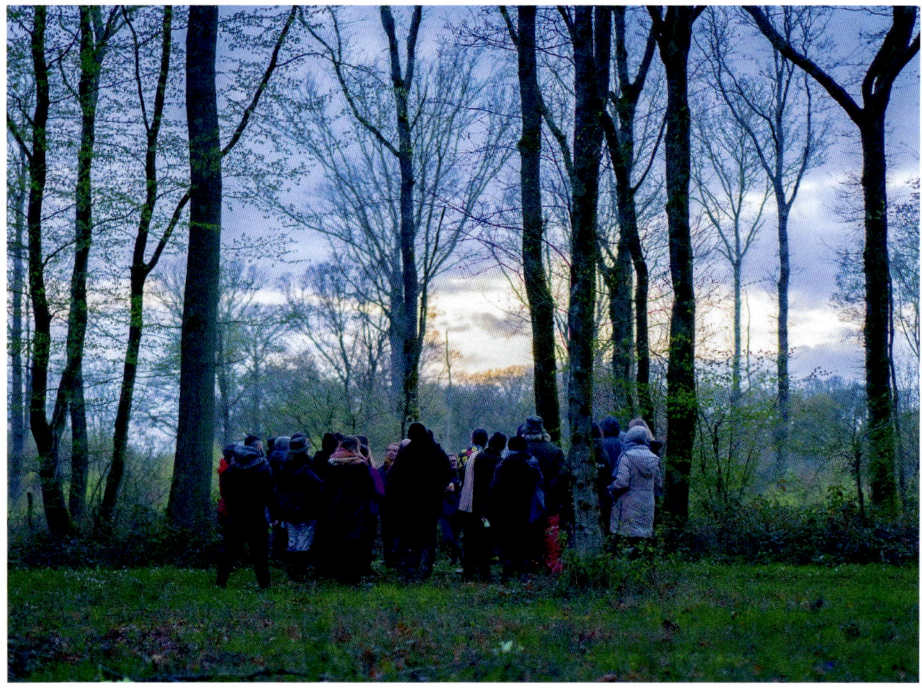

thousands across the south-east of England. The spring woods were once redolent with their famous courtship song, males exchanging improvised arias in collaborative, almost homoerotic, duets. Today this vital song has been mostly eradicated from our landscape with just 5,000 or so pairs left and those survivors in steep decline. This is due to the combined impacts of intensive agriculture, insect population collapse, housing developments destroying their habitats wholesale, but most of all a ballooning deer population ravishing and eating back new woodland growth across England.

This song was more than just a familiar feature but an essential symbol of the lifecycle that twinned us to the land. The nightingales have woven themselves into our folk songs, our art songs, our balladry and ancient prose, taking on archetypal characters as reminders, affirmers even, that we are nature and nature is us. This is not just specific to England either. Although never breeding, only occasionally overshooting the borders on their spring migration, these birds have developed reputations in Wales, Scotland, Cornwall and even Ireland, a notoriety

Singing With Nightingales, Sussex, 2024. Photograph by Ollie Denton.

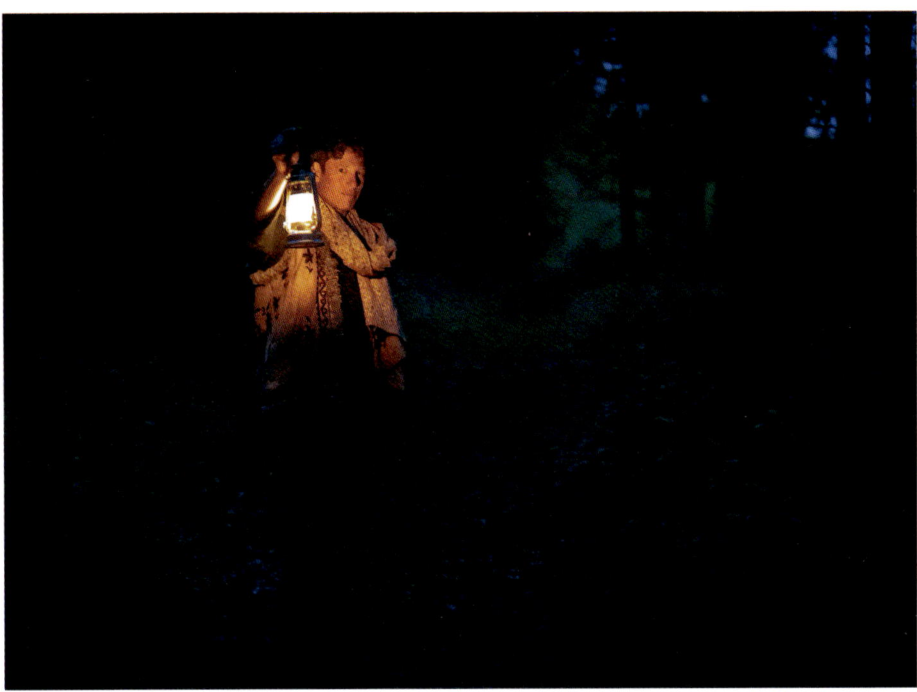

Sam Lee in the Sussex woods during the Singing With Nightingales season, 2023. Photograph by Ollie Denton.

that far precedes their habitat. Known as 'eos' in the Welsh and Cornish languages, many folk songs are sung adoringly in these westerly lands of their amorous role, revering a bird that would likely never have been heard by the singers, only talked of, as if from another world.

Globally speaking, England is their most westerly breeding territory. They will travel as far east as Western Mongolia and as far west as East Devon, spending the majority of their year in the West African coast river scrubs. Our wintering English birds will wander between Senegal, Sierra Leone and the Gambia, feeding as they move. But a twitch of the feather is felt around late February when they make the over-6,000-mile migration (alongside our other beloved birds such as cuckoos and blackcaps), to make landfall on English shores around early April. The males lead the charge, returning dutifully to the very blackthorn in which they were born, using their song to 'inform' other males of their location. By night, their 90-decibel song reaches high into the night sky like a sonic indicator to alert the females, who migrate later on, of where to find potential love.

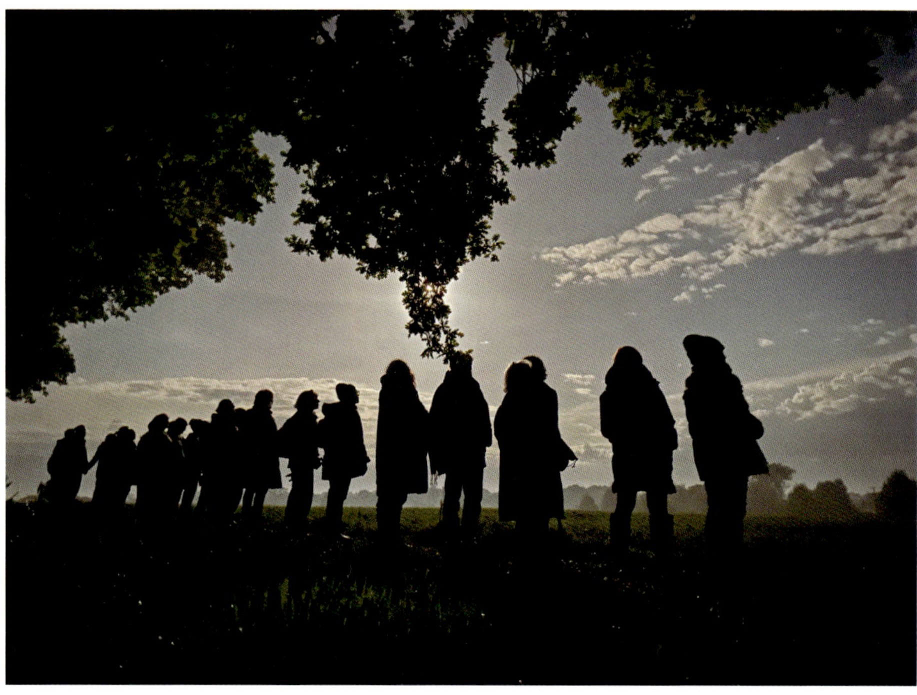

Singing With Nightingales, Sussex, 2024.
Photograph by Sam Lee.

Their song, comprising 1,200 unique sounds and up to 250 phrases, is a thesis on decoration and improvisation. Since the first instruments were crafted – bird-bone flutes made from swans and vulture leg bones excavated in German caves from at least 43,000 years ago – their song has been marvelled at by our ancestors. These proto-musicians were no doubt fascinated by this visceral and decorative song, a sound that, after sustained hearing, can send listeners into a trance. That same quality was aspired to as we began to work with altered states within proto-religious ceremonies. As these flourished, so did our dexterous ability to imitate our natural soundscape, and nightingales would have been the great teacher for our ancestors. Today that same role is still found within many folk traditions. In Afghanistan, players of the national instrument, the rabab, will acquire the acclaim of 'master musician' if, while out by night in the fig groves playing their instruments, the nightingale, locally named 'bulbul', flies onto the rabab's tuning pegs and sings along.

This collaborative nature of nightingales to respond and adapt their song in musical accordance to human musicians has

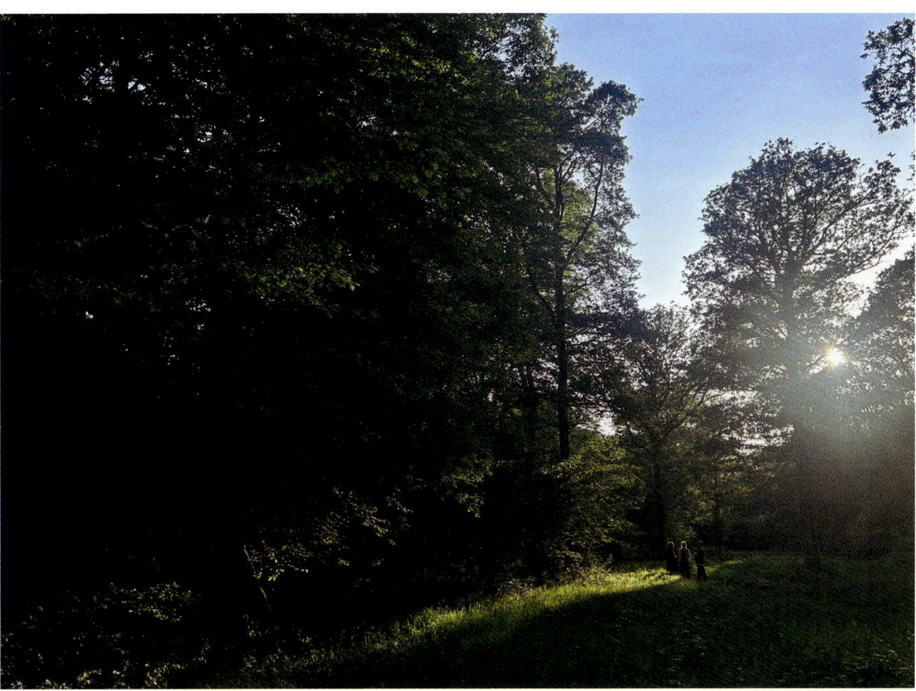

Singing With Nightingales, Sussex, 2024.
Photograph by Simon Martin.

great precedence. It is a phenomenon much adored across their habitat range, but one that in 1924 made history in the UK in a duet that pioneered outside-of-the-studio radio broadcasting. On 19 May, the legendary cellist and muse of Elgar, Beatrice Harrison, famously played her cello with the nightingale; it was listened to across the world on the wireless and brought what was by then an already much-forgotten song back into public awareness. Almost 100 years later, it was while honouring this historic moment during one of my Singing With Nightingale concert series – where I take musicians and audiences out into the dark to experience this phenomenon – that Maggi Hambling was initiated. Falling on the auspicious night of Earth Day 2023, Maggi, brought as a guest by her friends, was introduced to this ritual and celebration of nature. The transgressive thrill of walking into the night and experiencing nature and humans in sublime collaboration is indescribable, but when great artists meet, great art emerges and Maggi's ensuing body of work is a daring and unique response to one of nature's most forgotten phenomena.

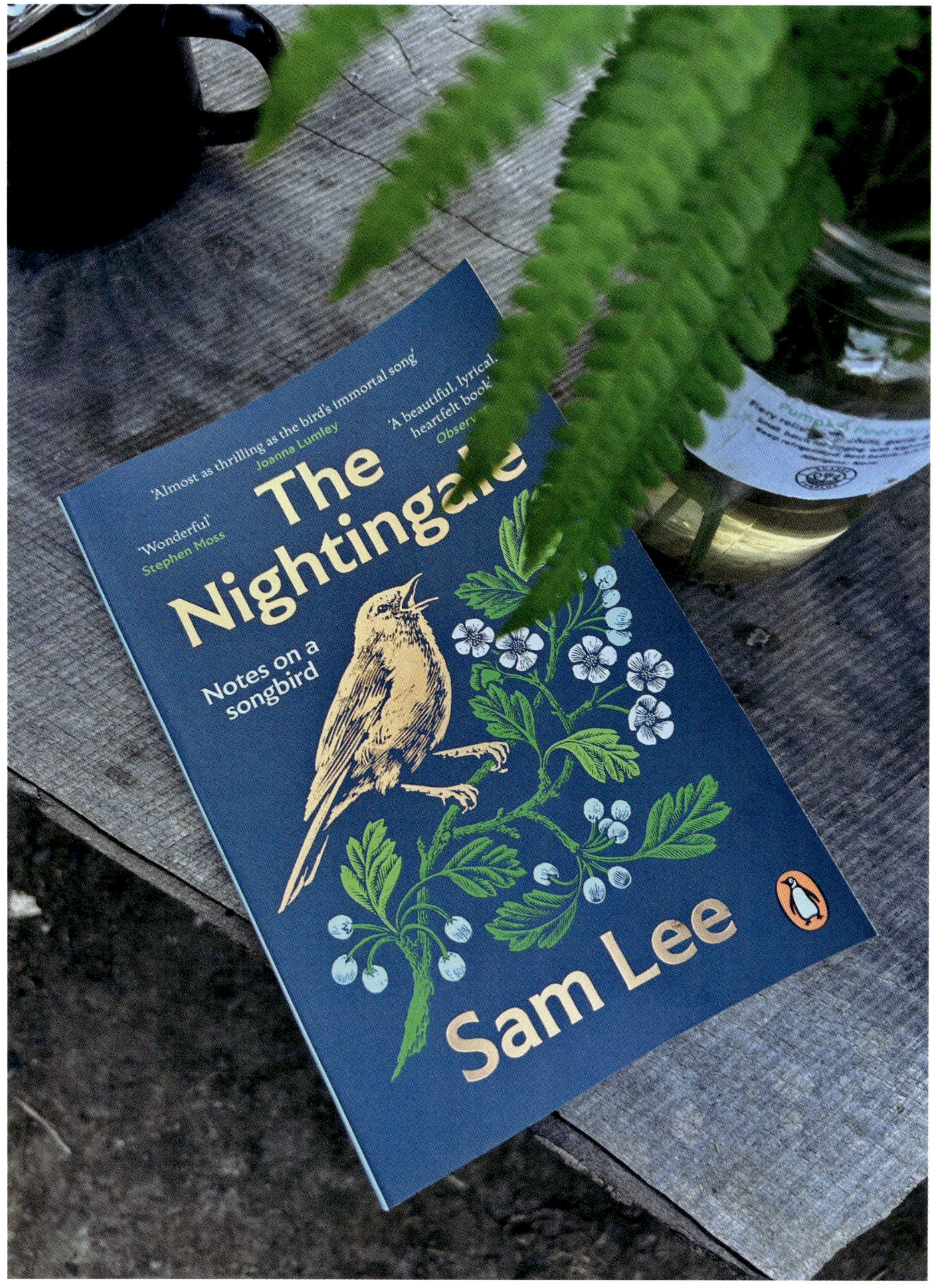
'Almost as thrilling as the bird's immortal song'
Joanna Lumley
'A beautiful, lyrical, heartfelt book'
Observer
'Wonderful'
Stephen Moss
The Nightingale
Notes on a songbird
Sam Lee

Despite the vitality found in both the bird's song and Maggi's artworks alike, there is melancholy within this encounter and its response. Nightingales are a barometer of the health of the land, but also our own connection and kinship to nature. As a red-list endangered species, they hold the unfortunate role of being one of the next birds we expect to see disappear from our shores, driven to extinction and falling silent, likely within the next 20 years. This book, and the works within, therefore mark a terrifying possibility as being among the last expressions of lived human devotion towards this species. Maybe these tones of tragedy Maggi offers are an opportunity for resolute defiance – a salutary reminder of art's vital purpose in reminding us what in life is truly essential and maybe what needs to be held in higher regard.

We cannot protect what we do not love, and we cannot love what we do not know. Maggi Hambling's paintings offer us a splendid opportunity to know the nightingale in ways never before told. Through these beacons in the dark, we are channelled into the wistful and lustful ways of a bird whose own art we may soon find ourselves becoming the last generation privileged in hearing.

Sam Lee, *The Nightingale.*
Photograph by Simon Martin.

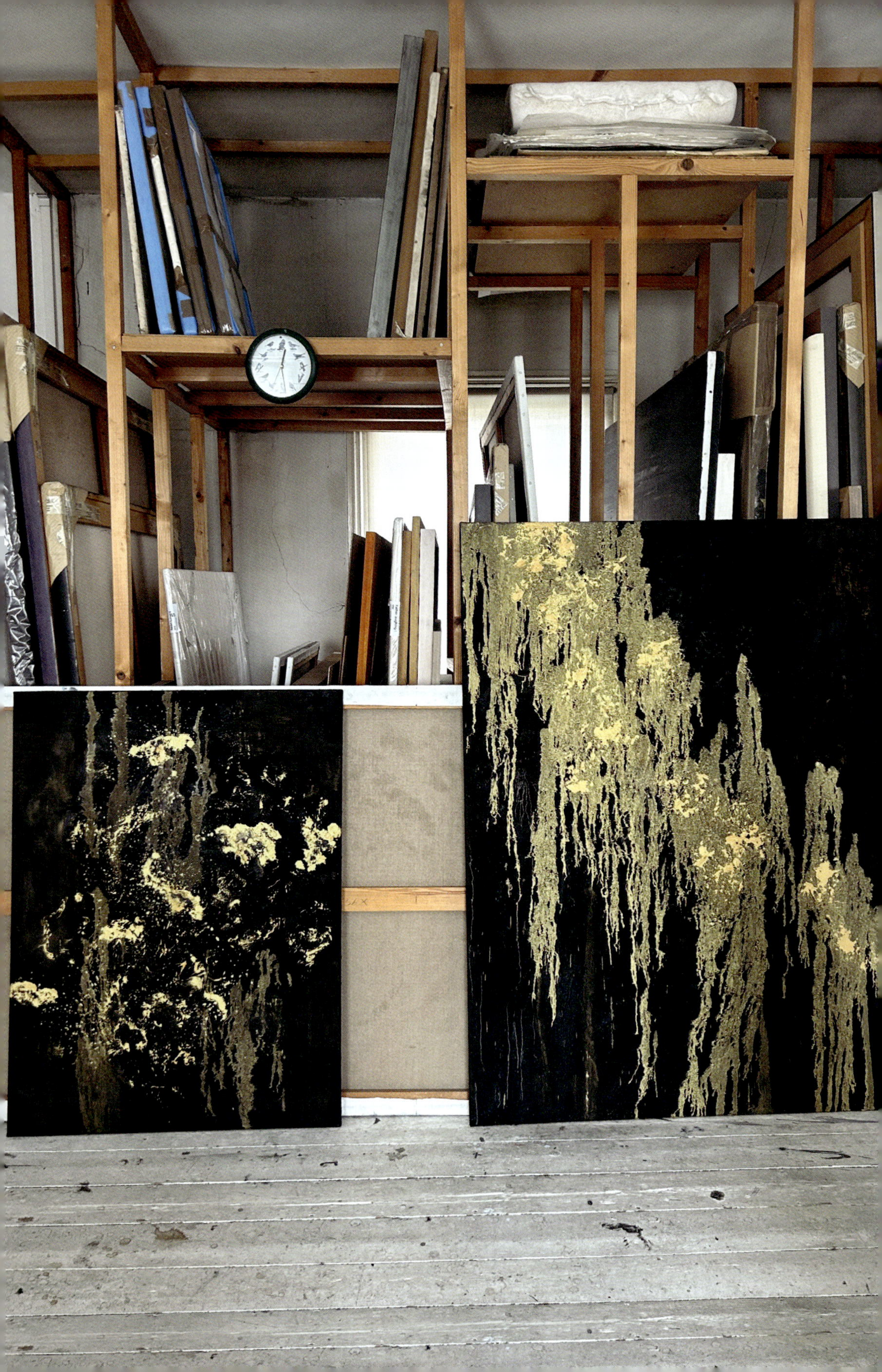

Paintings

Maggi Hambling's London studio, 2024.
Photograph by Simon Martin.

Maggi Hambling

Nightingale night I, 2023
Oil on canvas, 121.9 x 91.4 cm

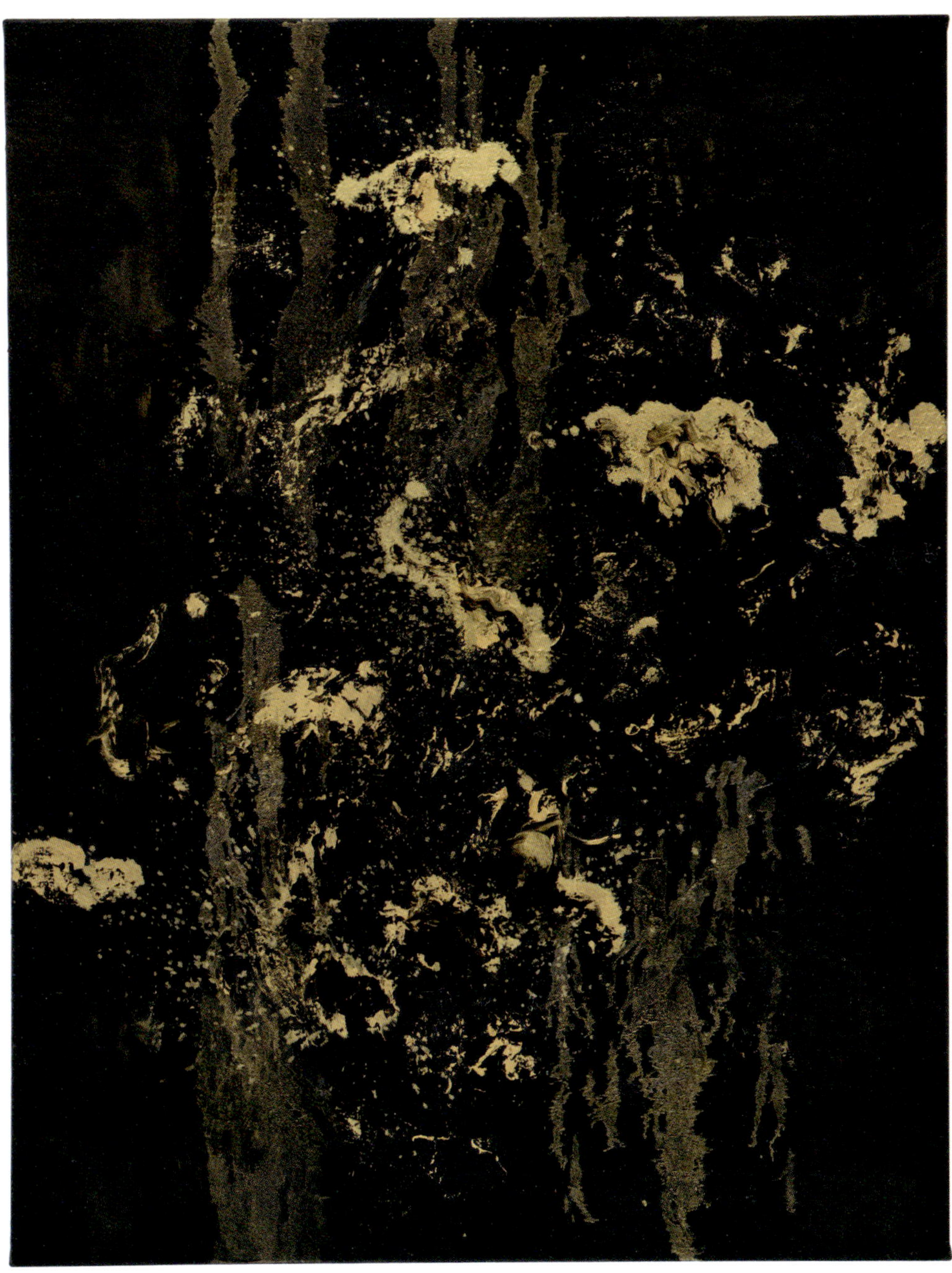

Maggi Hambling

Nightingale night II, 2023
Oil on canvas, 121.9 x 91.4 cm

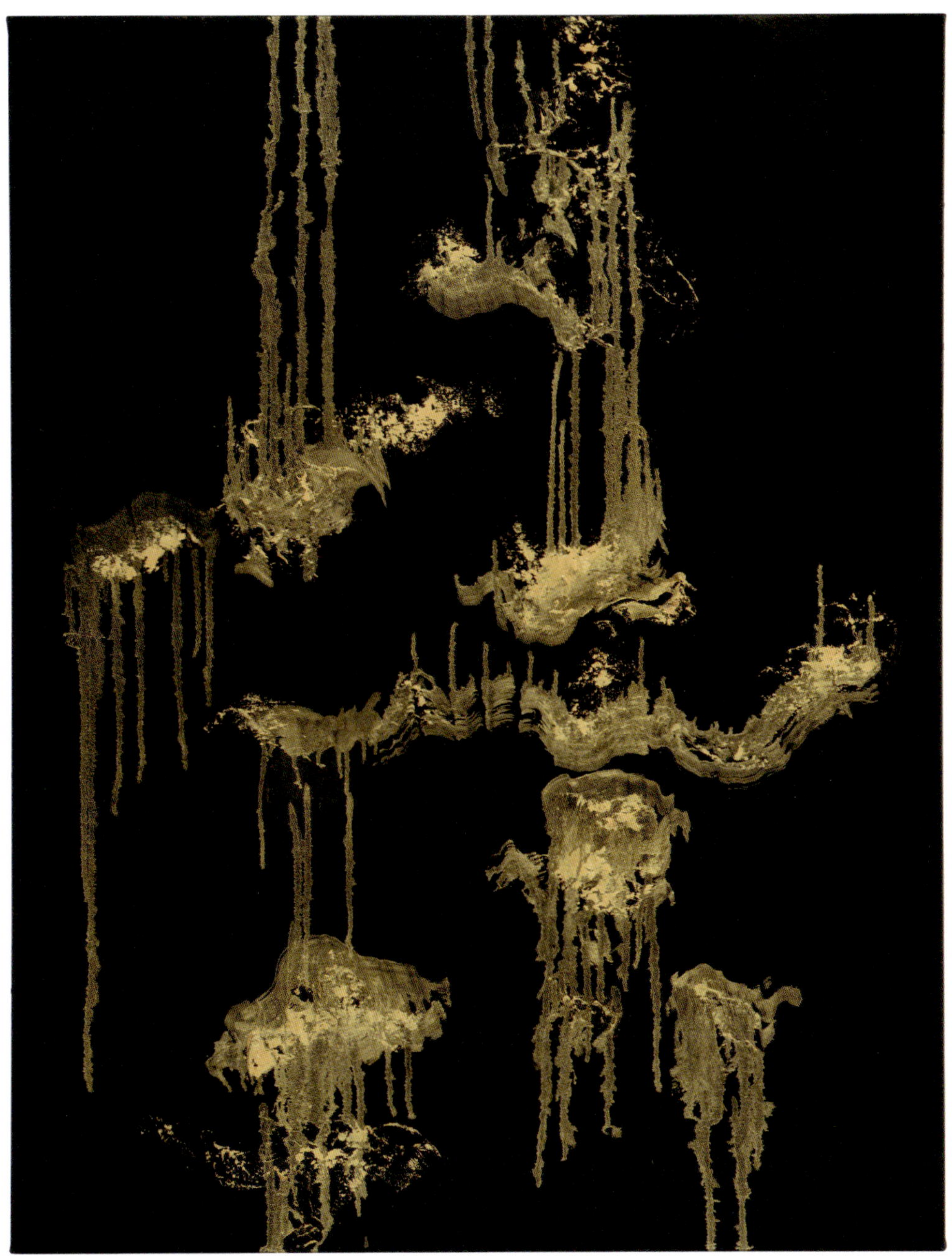

Maggi Hambling

Nightingale night III, 2023
Oil on canvas, 170.2 x 121.9 cm

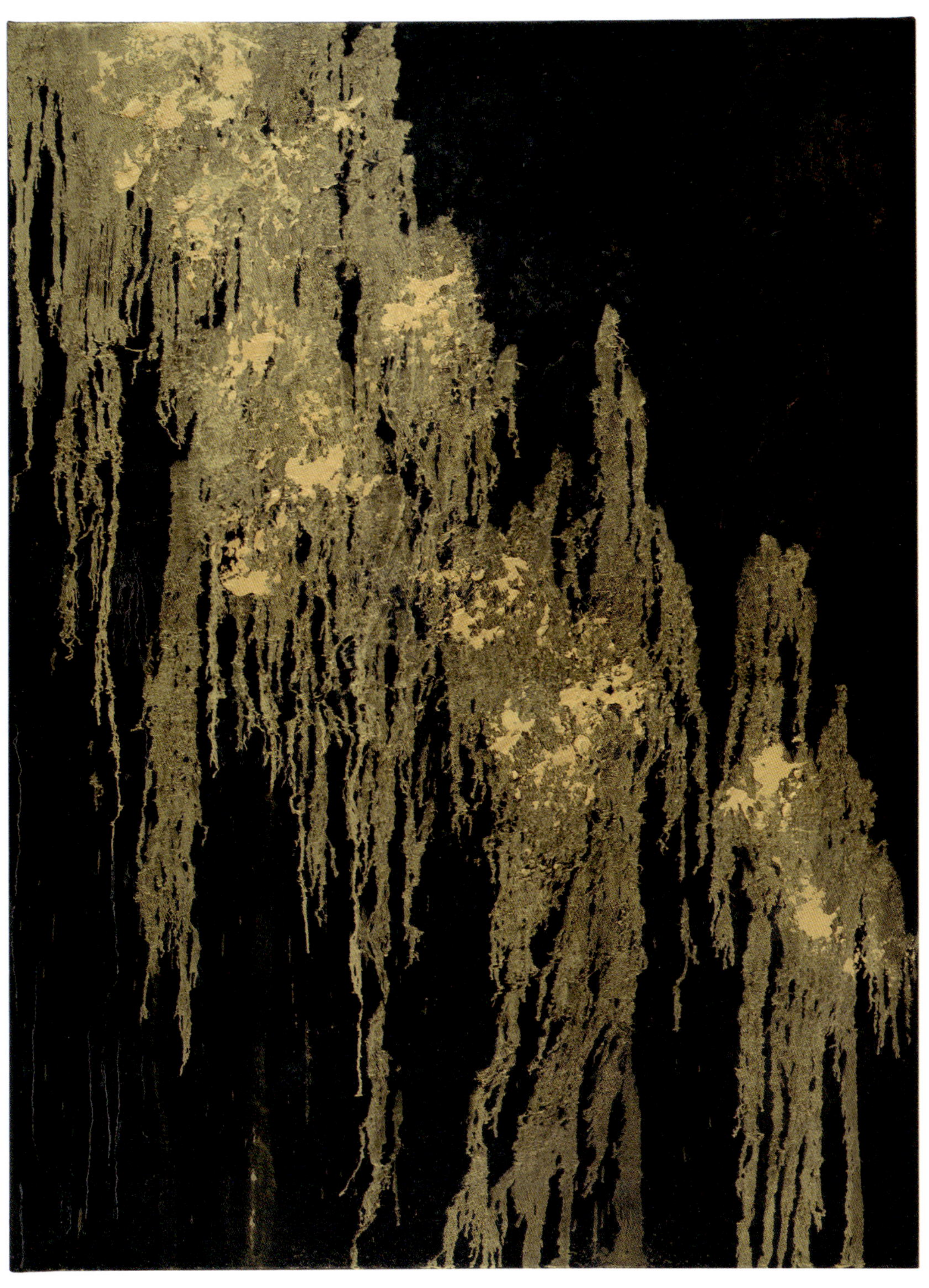

Maggi Hambling

Nightingale night IV, 2023
Oil on canvas, 30.5 x 25.4 cm

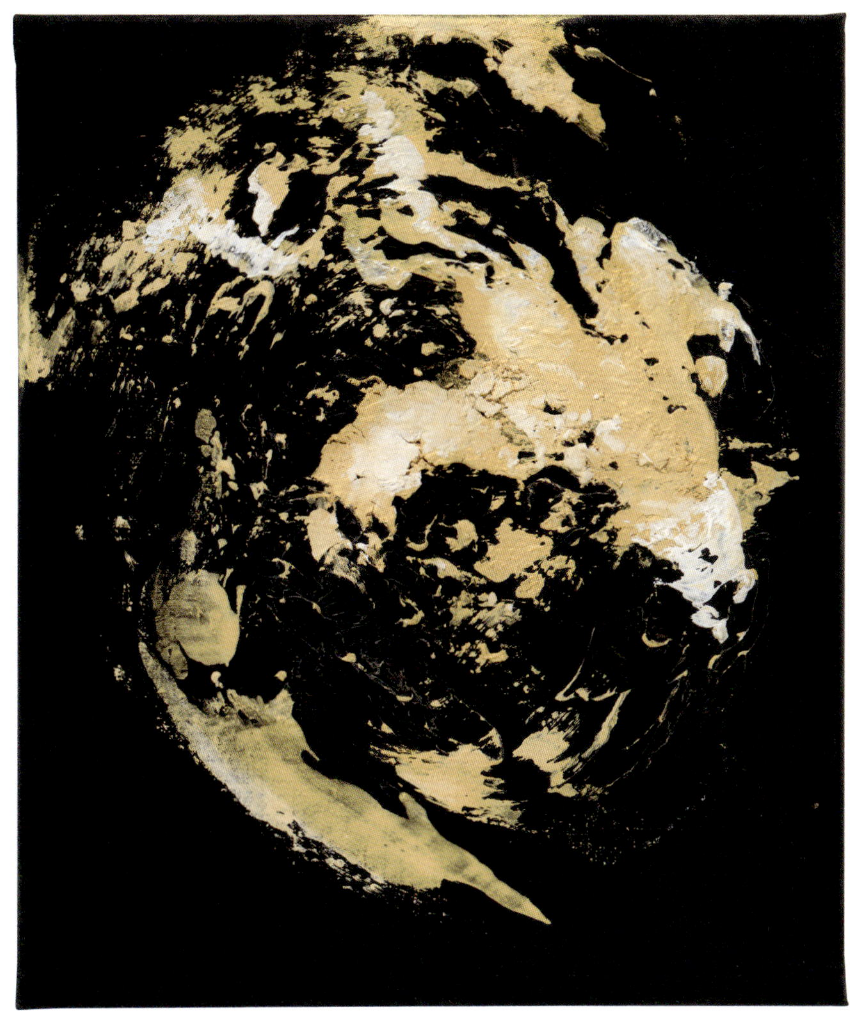

Maggi Hambling

Nightingale night V, 2023
Oil on canvas, 59.7 x 40.6 cm

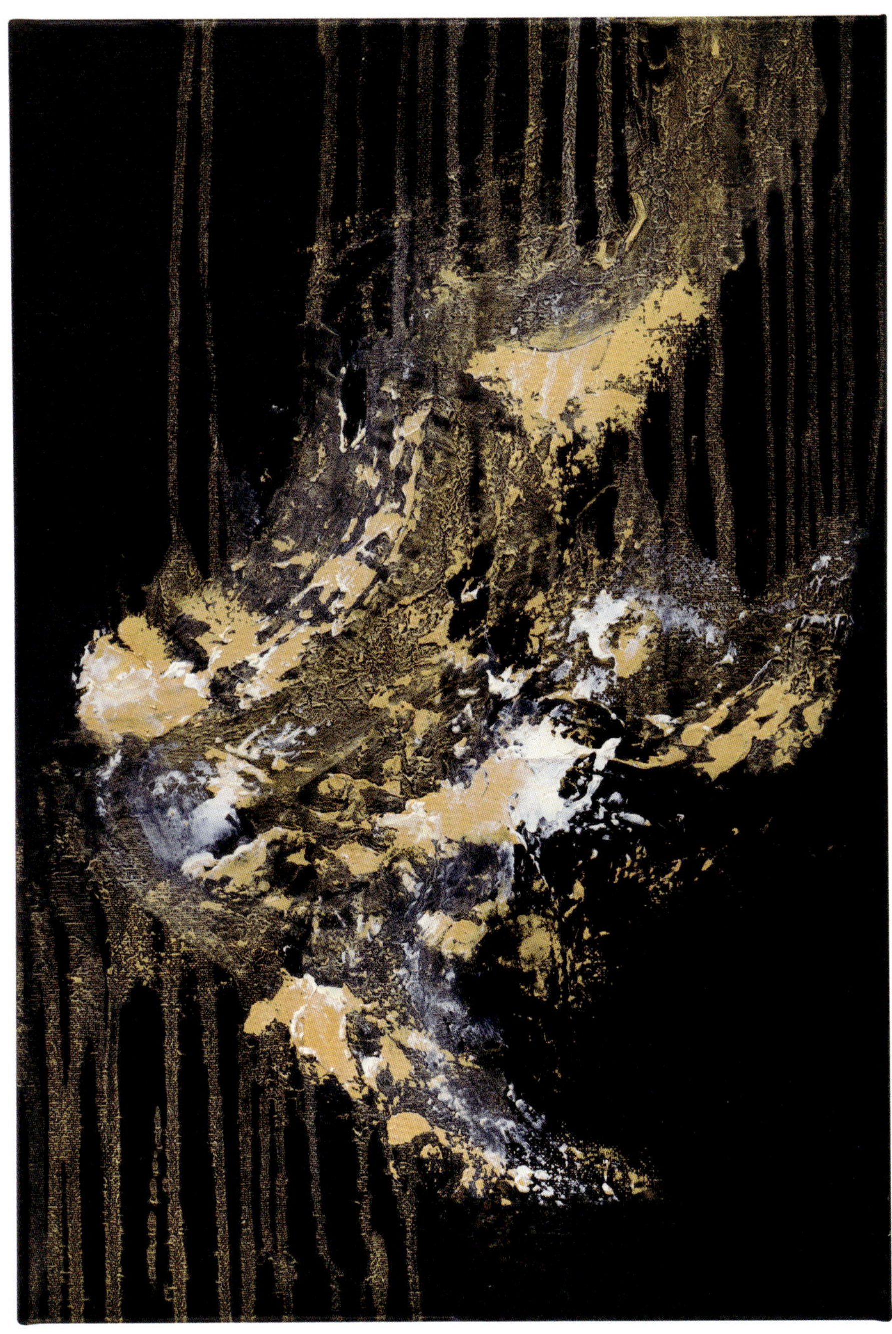

Maggi Hambling

Nightingale night VI, 2023
Oil on canvas, 53.3 x 43.2 cm

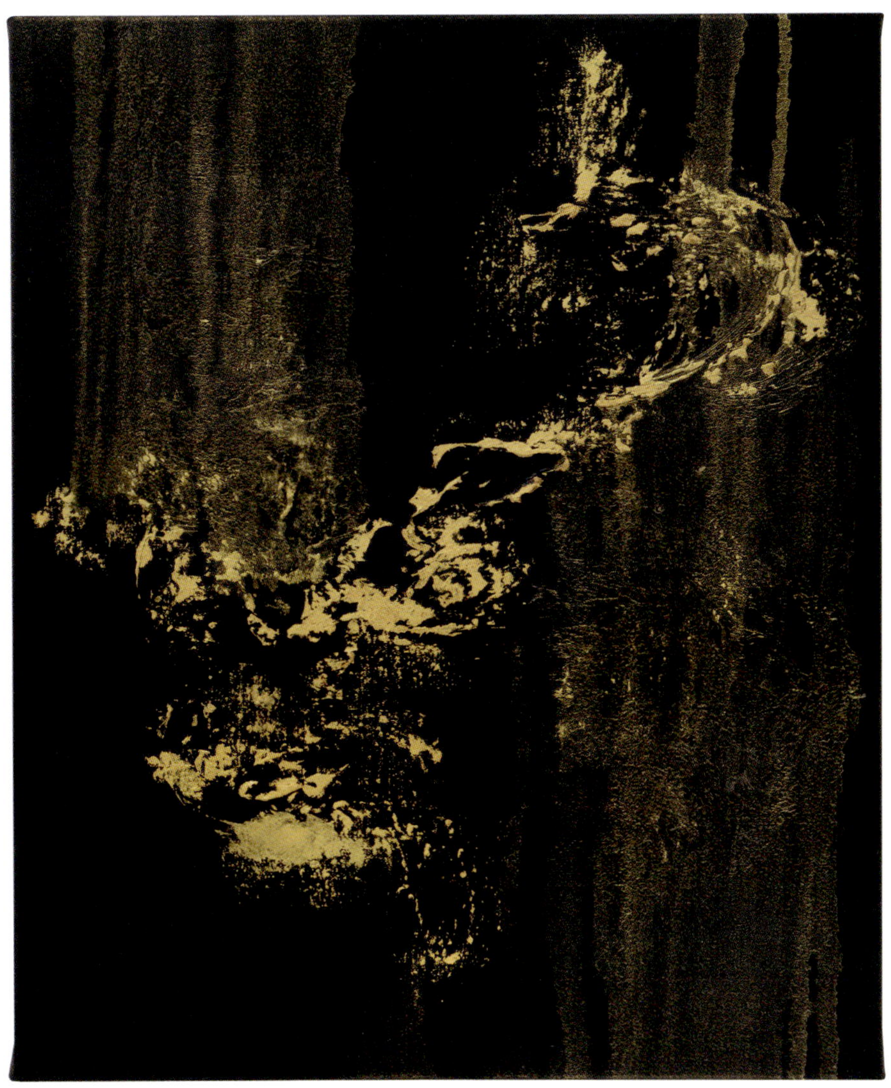

Maggi Hambling

Nightingale night VII, 2023
Oil on canvas, 40.6 x 61.0 cm

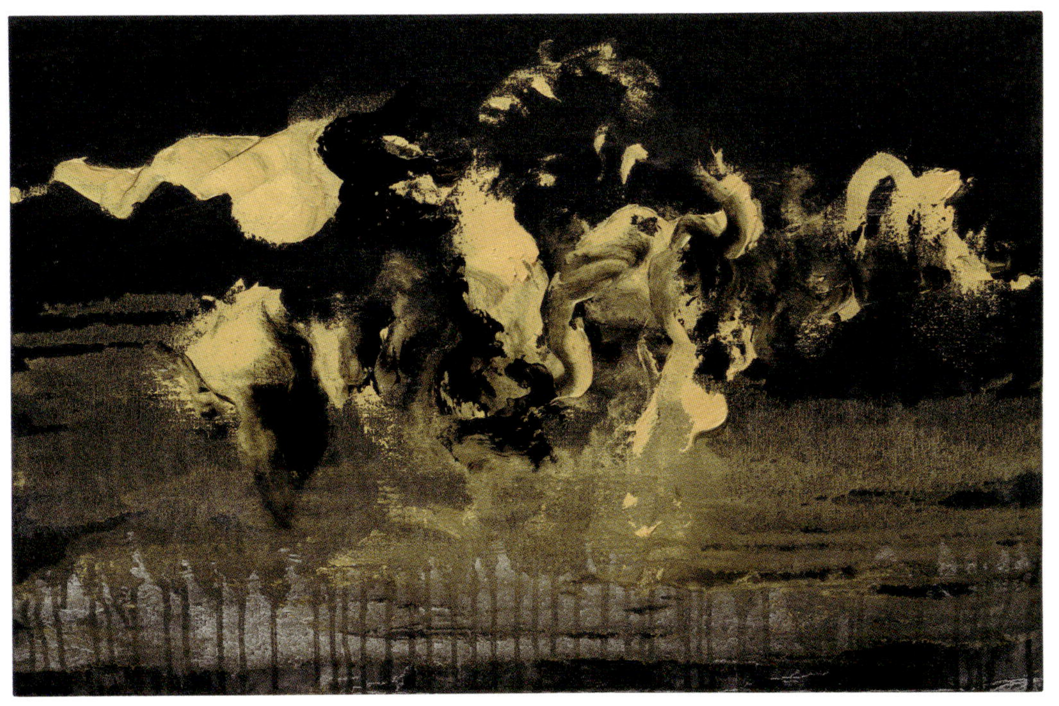

Maggi Hambling

Nightingale night VIII, 2023–24
Oil on canvas, 213.4 x 91.4 cm

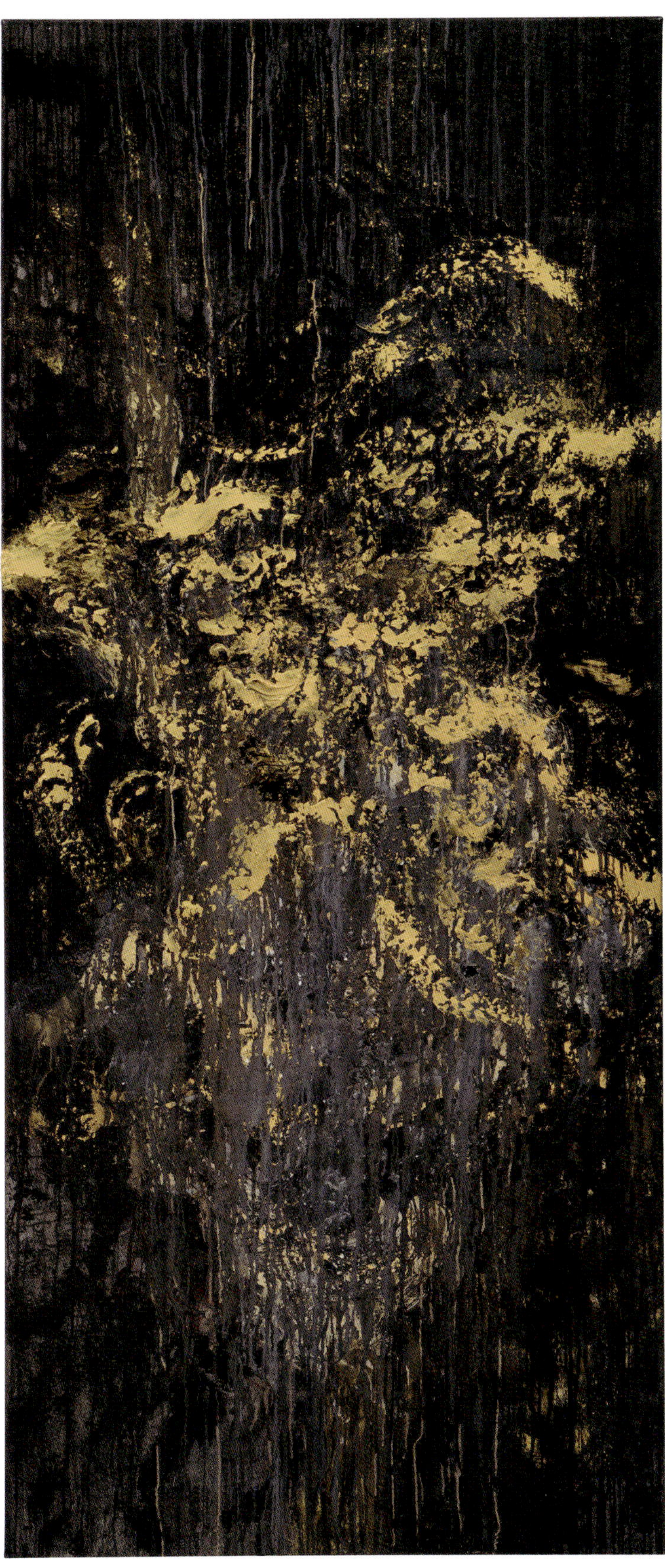

Maggi Hambling

Nightingale night IX, 2024
Oil on canvas, 182.9 x 91.4 cm

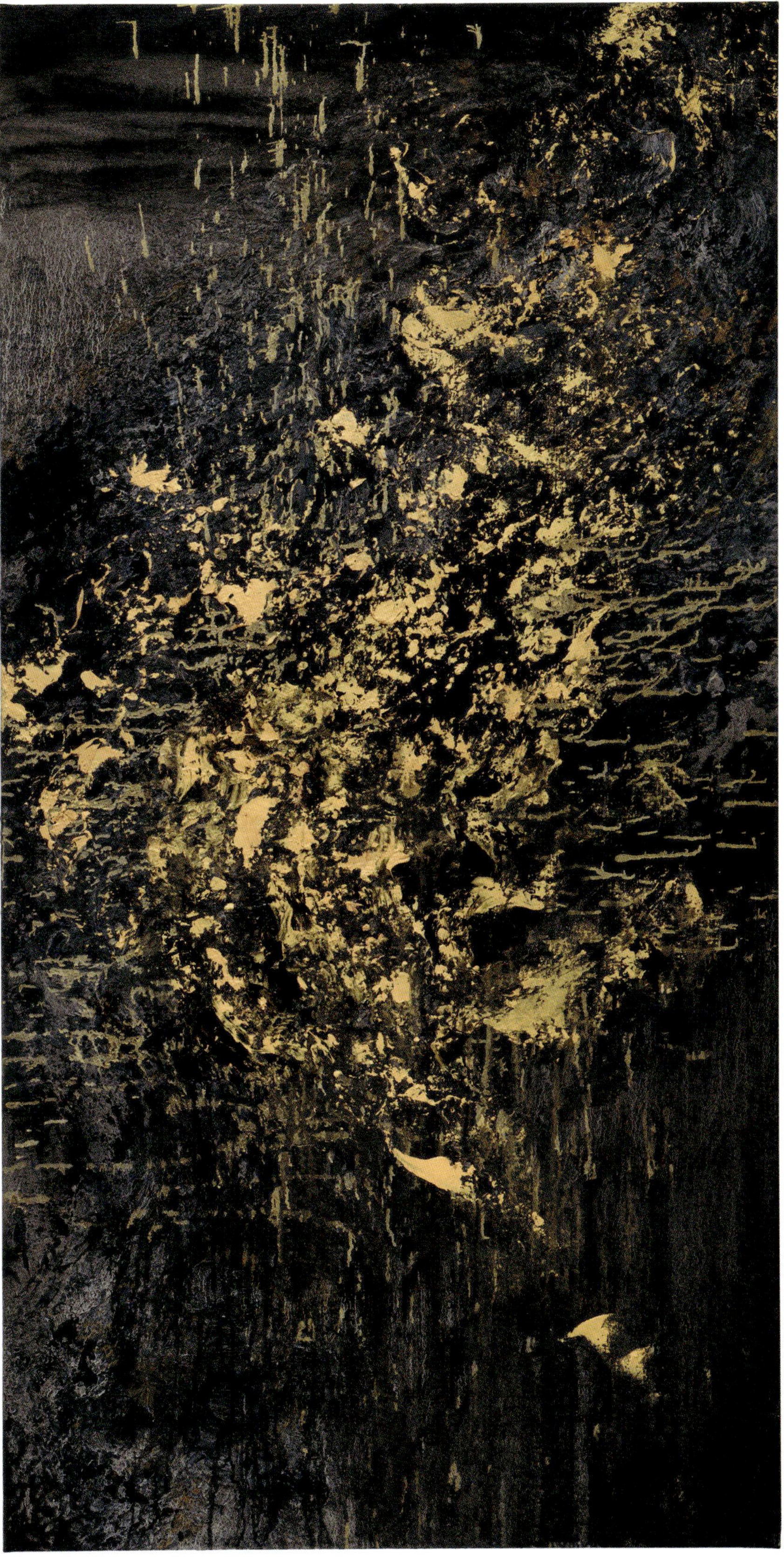

Maggi Hambling

Nightingale night X, 2024
Oil on canvas, 78.7 x 30.5 cm

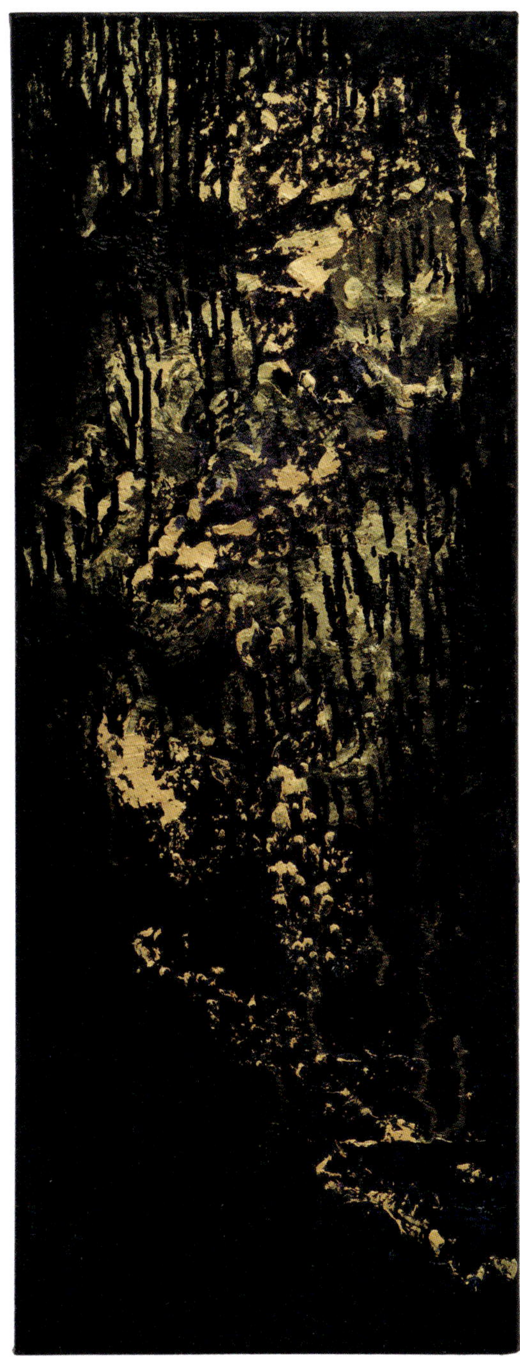

Maggi Hambling

Nightingale night XI, 2024
Oil on canvas, 80 x 30.5 cm

Maggi Hambling

Nightingale night XII, 2024
Oil on canvas, 53.3 x 43.2 cm

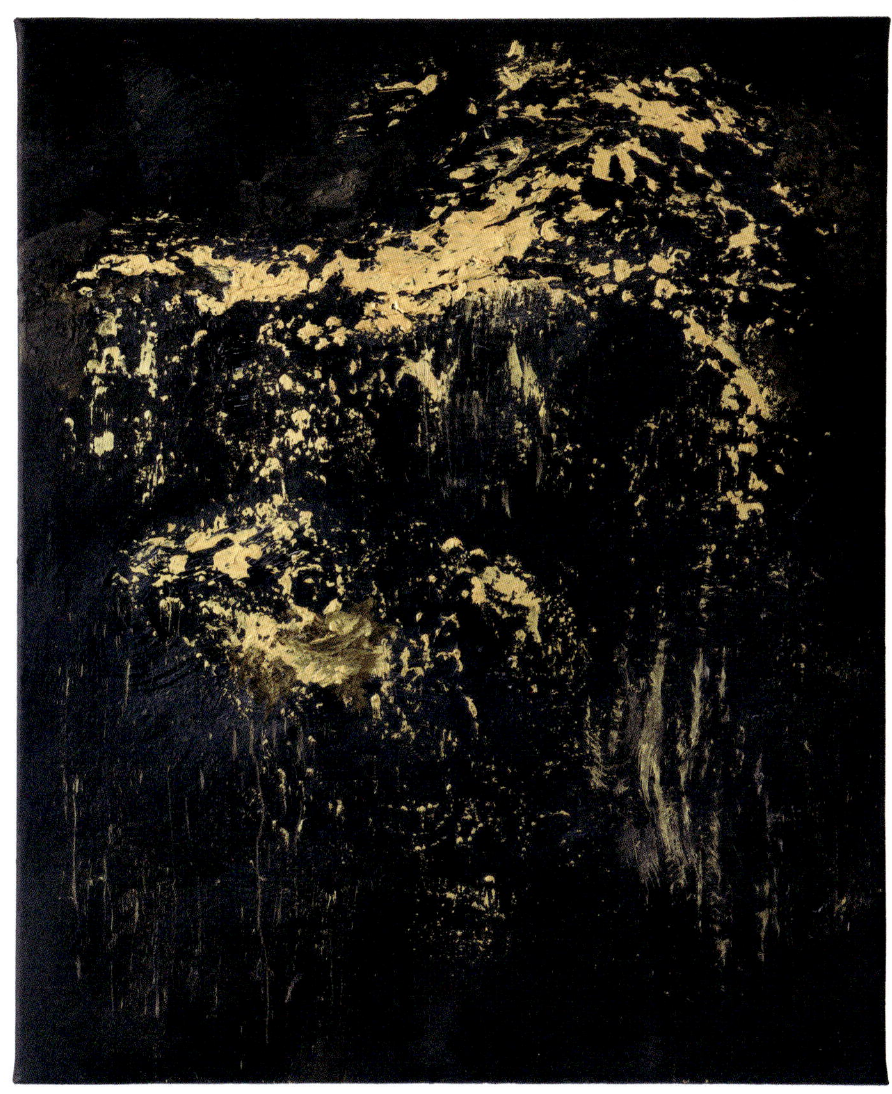

Maggi Hambling

Nightingale night XIII, 2024
Oil on canvas, 30.5 x 25.4 cm

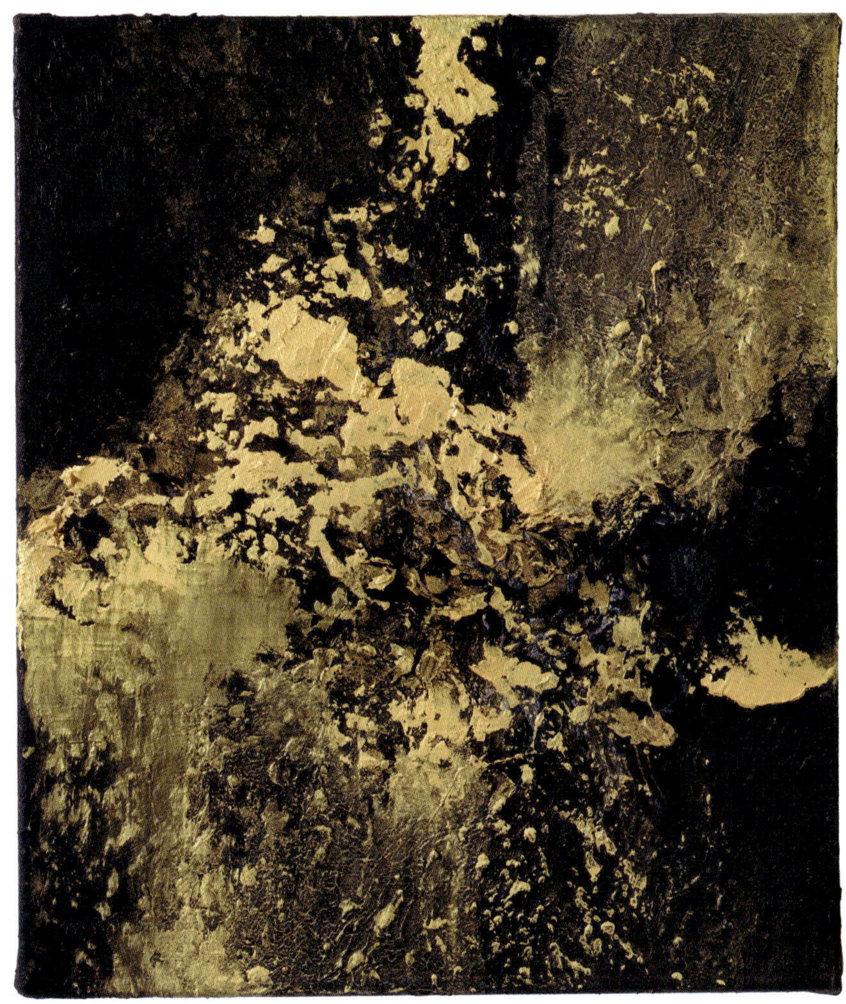

Maggi Hambling

74

Nightingale night XIV, 2024
Oil on canvas, 40.6 x 61.0 cm

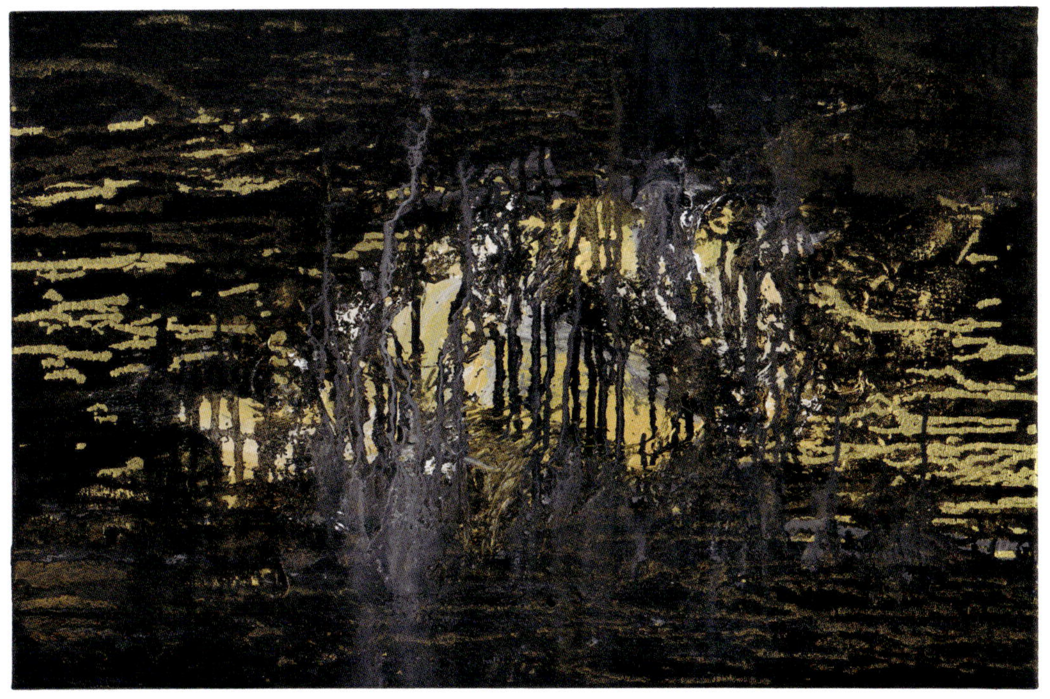

Maggi Hambling

Listening to nightingales I, 2023
Oil on canvas, 43.2 x 53.3 cm

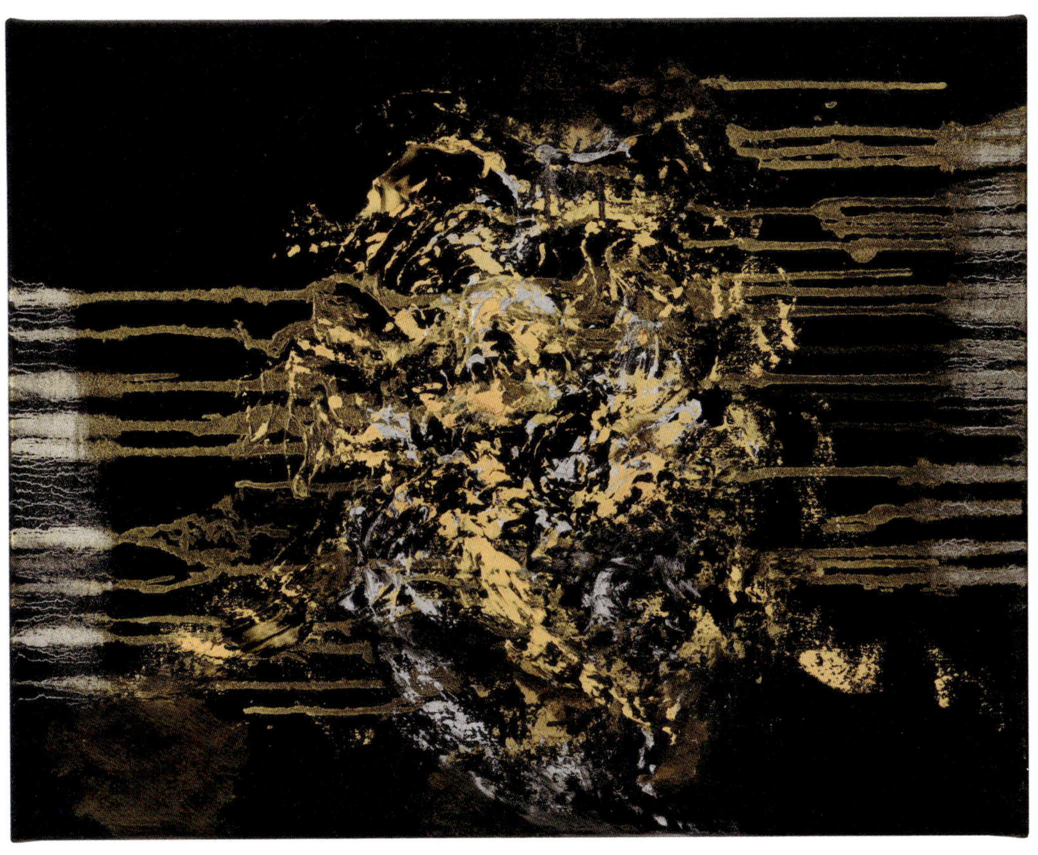

Maggi Hambling

Listening to nightingales II, 2023
Oil on canvas, 53.3 x 42.2 cm

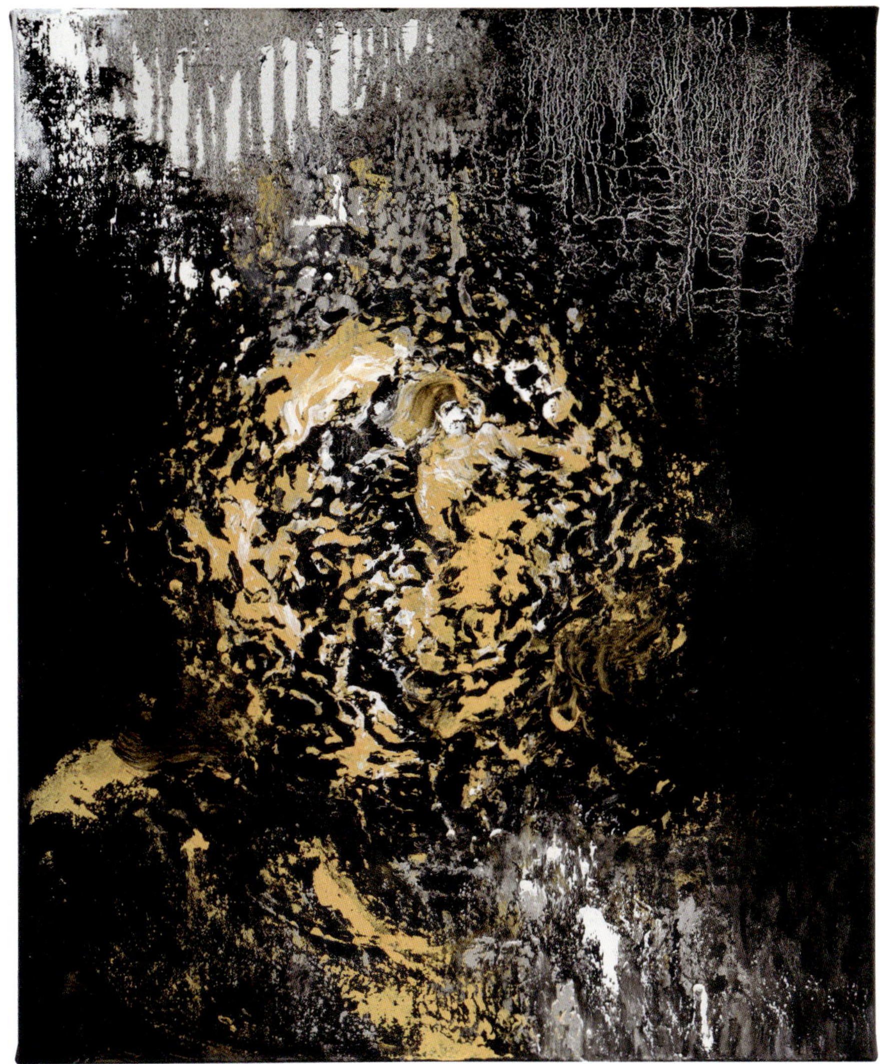

Leonard Cohen, 2016–17
Oil on canvas, 152.4 x 121.9 cm

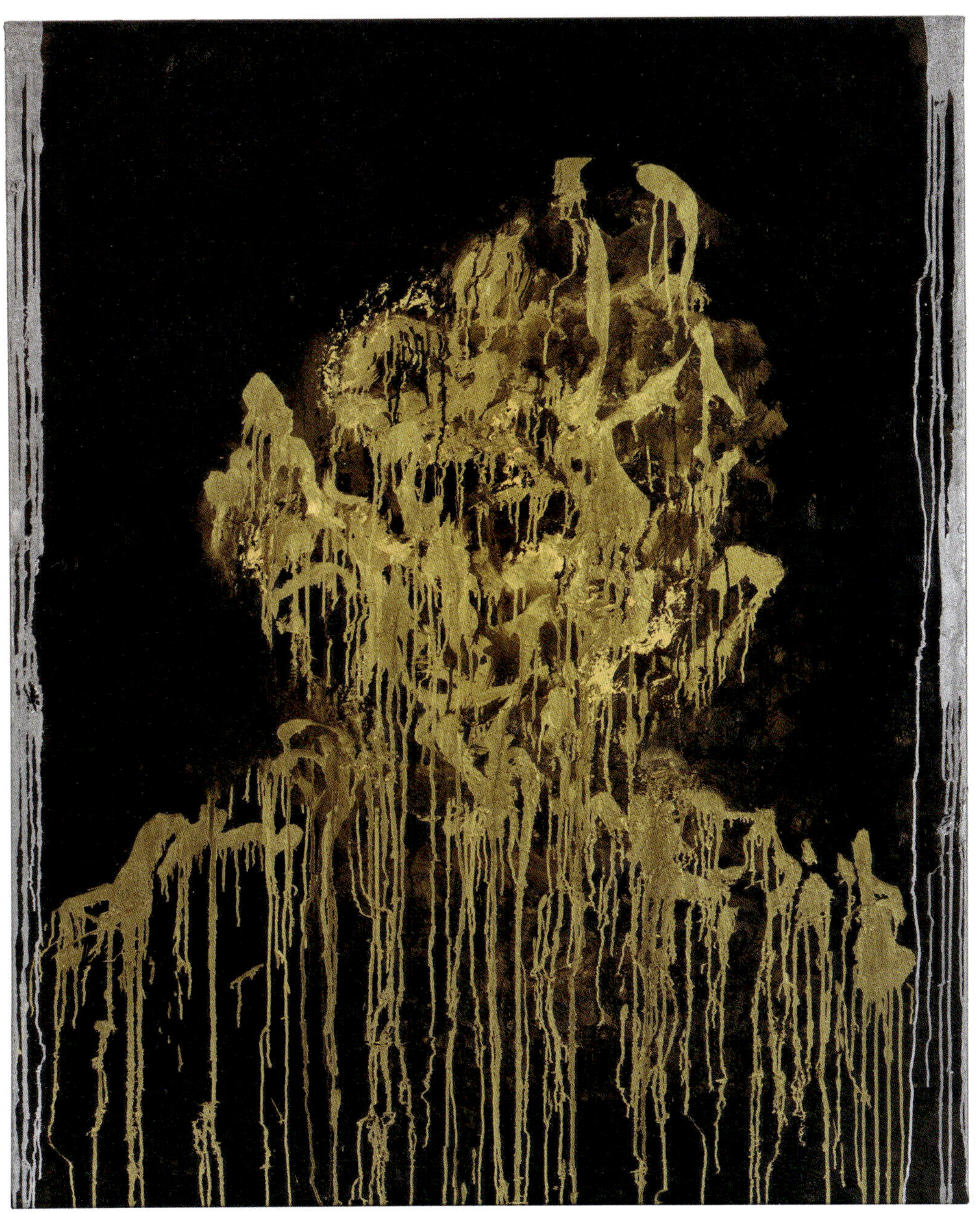

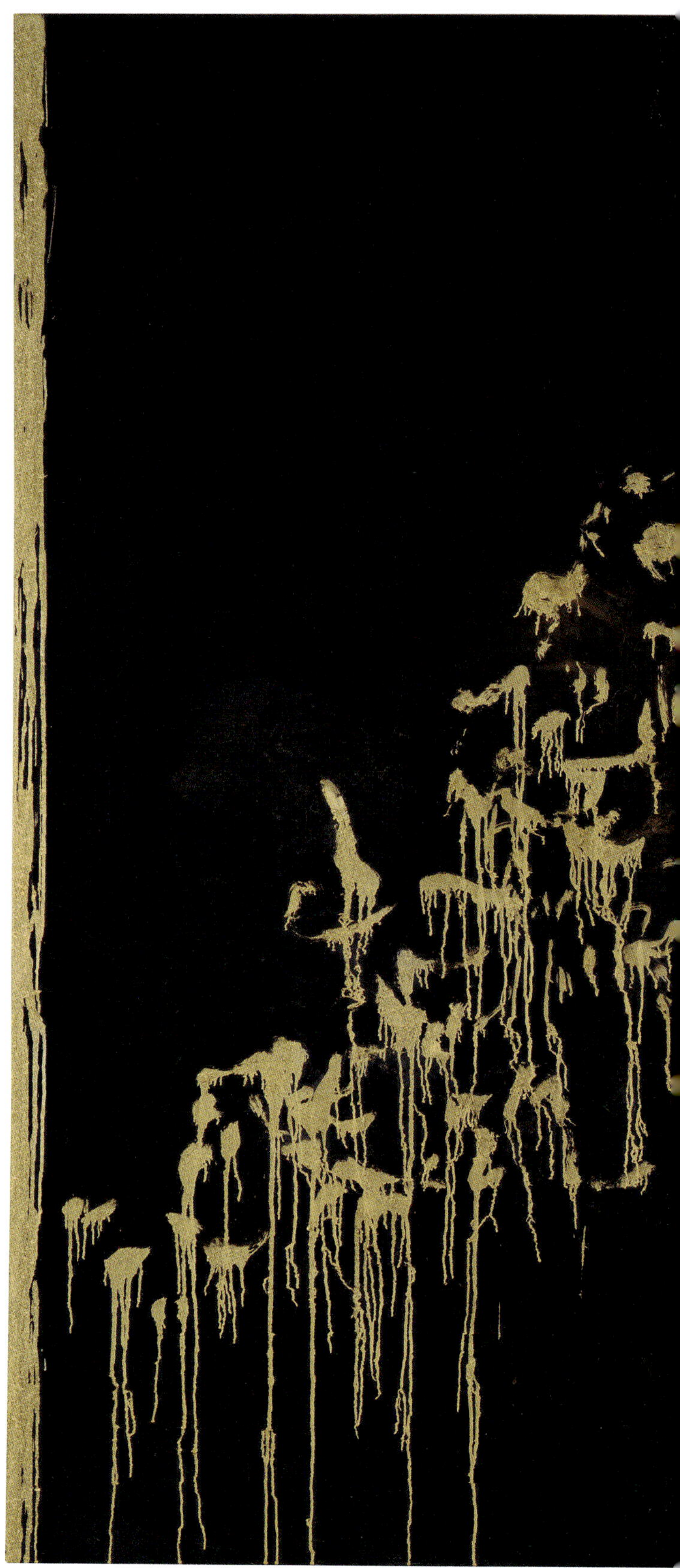

Night of the Lotus Eaters, 2019
Oil on canvas, 198.1 x 226.1 cm

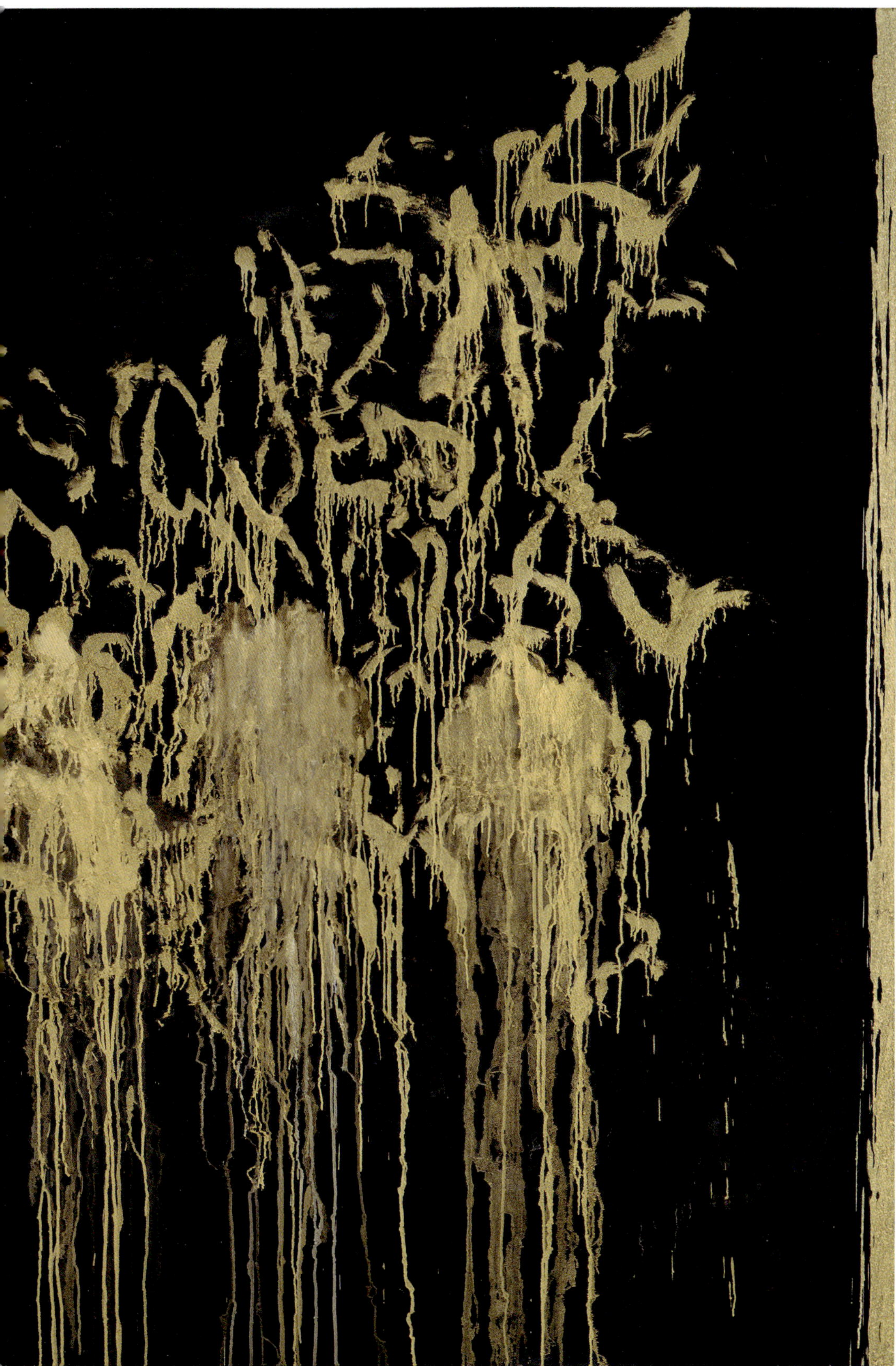

Maggi Hambling

Will Young, 2024
Oil on canvas, 53.4 x 43.2 cm (diptych)

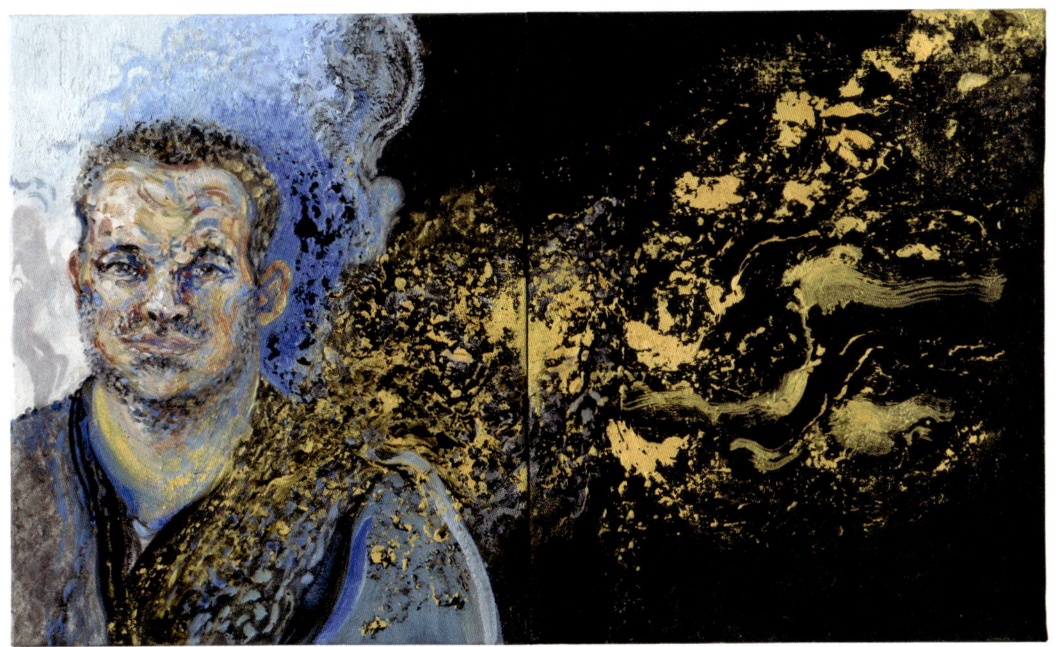

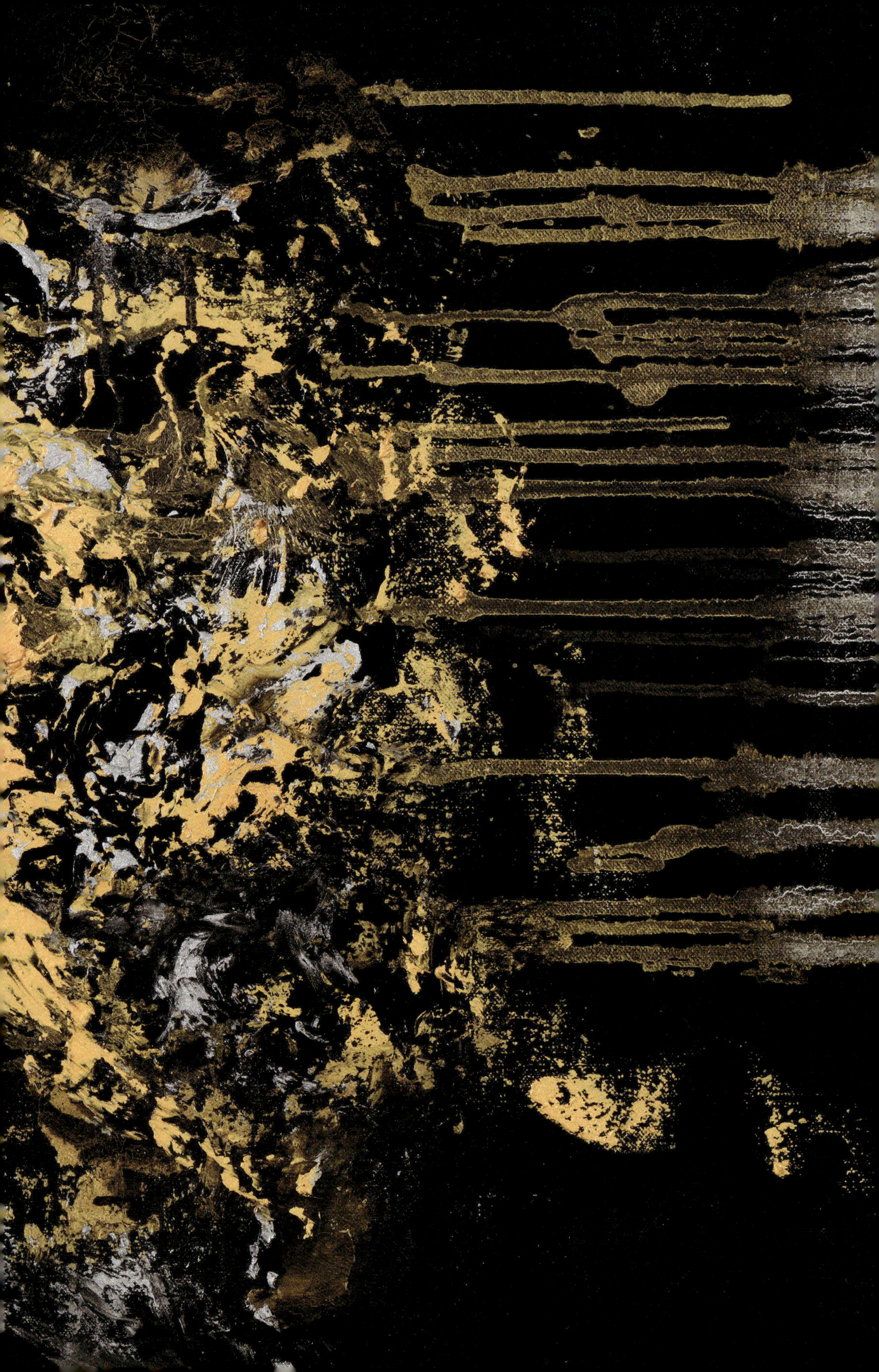

Biography

Nightingale night I, 2023 (detail)
Oil on canvas, 121.9 x 91.4 cm

Maggi Hambling

Note: all locations are in the United Kingdom unless stated otherwise.

1945	Born in Sudbury, Suffolk
	The artist lives and works in London and Suffolk

Education

1960	With Cedric Morris and Lett Haines at the East Anglian School of Paintings and Drawing
1962–64	Studied at Ipswich School of Art, Suffolk
1964–67	Studied at Camberwell School of Art, London
1967–69	Studied at Slade School of Fine Art, London

Solo Exhibitions

2024	*Maggi Hambling: The Night*, Pearl Lam, Hong Kong
2023	*Maggi Hambling: On the Edge*, Museo Ettore Fico, Turin, Italy
	Maggi Hambling: Maelstrom, Hazlitt Holland-Hibbert, London
	Maggi Hambling 4AM, Galería Marlborough, Madrid, Spain
2022	*Maggi Hambling: Real Time*, Marlborough Gallery, New York, USA
	Maggi Hambling: Glyndebourne, Glyndebourne, Lewes
2021	*RELIC*, Snape Maltings, Suffolk
2020	*Maggi Hambling: 2020*, Marlborough Gallery, London
2019	*Maggi Hambling: For Beauty is Nothing but the Beginning of Terror*, CAFA Art Museum, Beijing, China, travelled to Guangdong Museum, Guangzhou, China
2018	*New Portraits*, Marlborough Gallery, London
2017	*Edge*, Marlborough Gallery, London
2016	*Maggi Hambling, Touch: Works on Paper*, The British Museum, London
2015	*Maggi Hambling: War Requiem and Aftermath*, King's College, London

2014	*Maggi Hambling: Walls of Water*, The National Gallery, London
2013	*Wall of Water*, The Hermitage, St Petersburg, Russia
2010	*Maggi Hambling: The Wave*, Fitzwilliam Museum, Cambridge
	Maggi Hambling: Sea Sculpture – paintings and etchings, Marlborough Gallery
	Maggi Hambling's Self Portrait, Freud Museum, London
2009	*George Always – Portraits of George Melly by Maggi Hambling*, Walker Art Gallery, Liverpool
	Maggi Hambling: North Sea Paintings, New works on paper, The Gallery, Snape Maltings
2007	*Maggi Hambling: No Straight Lines*, Octagon Gallery, The Fitzwilliam Museum, Cambridge; travelled to Victoria Art Gallery, Bath; Abbot Hall Art Gallery, Kendal
	Maggi Hambling: Waves, Marlborough Gallery, London
	Maggi Hambling: Waves Breaking – paintings, Northumbria University Gallery, Newcastle upon Tyne
2006	*Maggi Hambling: Portraits of People and the Sea*, Marlborough Gallery, London
2004	*Maggi Hambling: Thorpeness Sluice & North Sea Waves*, Peter Pears Gallery, Aldeburgh
2003	*North Sea Paintings*, Aldeburgh Festival Exhibition, Suffolk
2001	*Good Friday – Paintings, Drawings & Sculpture 1965-2001*, Lady Margaret Hall, Oxford; travelled to Gainsborough's House, Sudbury
	Henrietta Moraes by Maggi Hambling, Drawings, Paintings and Bronzes, Marlborough Gallery, London
	Father - Drawings and Paintings, Morley College Gallery, London
1998	*A Conversation with Oscar Wilde*, Marlborough Gallery, London
1997	*Maggi Hambling – A Matter of Life and Death*, Bothy Gallery, Yorkshire Sculpture Park, Yorkshire
	A Statue for Oscar Wilde, National Portrait Gallery, London
1995	*Sculpture in Bronze 1993–95*, Marlborough Gallery, London
1993–4	*Towards Laughter, Maggi Hambling*, Northern Centre for Contemporary Art, Sunderland
1993	*Dragon Morning, Works in Clay*, CCA Galleries, London
1992	*The Jemma Series, Monotypes*, Bernard Jacobson Gallery, London

1991	*An Eye Through a Decade*, Yale Center for British Art, Newhaven, Connecticut, USA
1990	*New Paintings 1989–90*, Bernard Jacobson Gallery, London
1988	*Maggi Hambling*, Richard Demarco Gallery, Edinburgh; travelled to Maclaurin Art Gallery, Ayr
	Maggi Hambling: Moments of the Sun, Arnolfini Gallery, Bristol and tour
1987	*Maggi Hambling*, Serpentine Gallery, London
1983	*Pictures of Max Wall*, National Portrait Gallery, London and tour
1981	*Drawings and Paintings on View*, National Gallery, London
1977	*New Oil Paintings*, Warehouse Gallery, London
1973	*Paintings and Drawings*, Morley Gallery, London
1967	*Paintings and Drawings*, Hadleigh Gallery, Suffolk

Selected Group Exhibitions

2023	*Big Women*, Firstsite, Colchester
2021	*Summer Exhibition*, Marlborough Gallery, London
2018–19	*The Quick & the Dead*, Hastings Contemporary, Hastings
2015	*A Summer Exhibition*, Marlborough Gallery, London
2006	*Drawing Inspiration*, Abbot Hall Art Gallery, Kendal
2004	*Summer Exhibition*, Marlborough Gallery, London
2001	*Out of Line, Drawings from the Arts Council Collection*, Travelling Exhibition
	London International Small Print Biennale, Morley Gallery, London
	Behind the Mask, The Hatton Gallery, Newcastle; travelled to The Bowes Museum, Durham
	About Face – Get Your Head Around Sculpture, Croydon Clock Tower, London
	The Enduring Image, Abbot Hall Art Gallery, Kendal
2000–1	*Painting the Century: 101 Portrait Masterpieces 1900–2000*, National Portrait Gallery, London
1998	*Suffolk – A Female Focus*, Ipswich Museum, Suffolk
1996	*Head First – Portraits from the Arts Council Collection*, City Art Gallery, Leicester; travelled to Southampton City Art

	Gallery; Abbot Hall Gallery, Kendal, Hatton Gallery, Newcastle; Victoria Art Gallery, Bath; The Graves Art Gallery, Sheffield; Ferens Art Gallery, Hull
	Artaid '98, Edinburgh City Art Centre, Edinburgh
1997	*British Figurative Art, Part One: Painting – The Human Figure*, Flowers East, London
	Animals in Art, Harris Museum and Art Gallery, Preston
1994	*Here and Now*, Serpentine Gallery, London
1993	*Images of Christ*, St Paul's Cathedral, London
	The Portrait Now, National Portrait Gallery, London
1992	*Eighty Years of Collecting by The Contemporary Art Society*, Hayward Gallery, London and tour
	Life into Paint: British Figurative Painting of the 20th Century, British Council, Israel Museum, Jerusalem
1991	*Modern Painters*, Manchester City Art Gallery, Manchester
1990	*Nine Contemporary Painters*, City of Bristol Museum and Art Gallery
1989	*Within These Shores, A Selection of Works from the Chantrey Bequest 1883–1985*, Sheffield City Art Gallery
	Salute to Turner, Thomas Agnew & Sons, London
	Picturing People – British Figurative Art Since 1945, British Council, Malaya, Hong Kong and Singapore
1988	*Artists and National Parks*, Victoria and Albert Museum, London and tour
1987	*The Self Portrait*, Artsite, Bath and tour
1986	*Visual Aid for Band Aid*, Royal Academy, London
	Artist and Model, Whitworth Art Gallery, Manchester
	In Close Up, National Portrait Gallery, London
1985	*A Singular Vision*, Royal Albert Memorial Museum, Exeter
	In Their Circumstances, Usher Gallery, Lincoln
	Human Interest: 50 Years of British Art About People, Cornerhouse, Manchester
1984	*The Hard-Won Image*, Tate Gallery, London
1983	*Pintura Britanic Contemporanea*, Museo Municipal, Madrid, Spain
	3 Decades of Artists, Royal Academy, London
	Britain Salutes New York, Marlborough Gallery, New York, USA

1982	*Private Views*, Arts Council, touring exhibition
1981	*The Subjective Eye*, Midland Group, Nottingham and tour
1980	*British Art, 1940–80*, Hayward Gallery, London
1979	*Narrative Paintings*, Arnolfini Gallery, Bristol and tour
	The British Art Show, Mappin Art Gallery, Sheffield
1978	*6 British Artists*, British Council Drawing Exhibition, Yugoslavia
1976	*The Human Clay*, Hayward Gallery, London
1974	*Critic's Choice*, Tooths Gallery, London
	British Painting '74, Hayward Gallery, London
1973	*Artist's Market*, Warehouse Gallery, London

Awards / Residencies

1995	Jerwood Painting Prize
1980–1	First Artist in Residence, National Gallery, London
1977	Arts Council Award, London

Selected Commissions and Public Sculptures

2020	*A sculpture for Mary Wollstonecraft*, Newington Green, London
2013	*The Winchester Tapestries*, unveiled Winchester Cathedral, Hampshire
	The Resurrection Spirit, unveiled at St Dunstan's Church, Mayfield, East Sussex
2010	*The Brixton Heron*, London
2001	*Scallop (for Benjamin Britten)*, unveiled on Aldeburgh beach, Suffolk
1998	*A conversation with Oscar Wilde*, London

Monographs and Selected Exhibition Catalogues

2016	*Maggi Hambling, Touch: Works on Paper* (exh.cat.), The British Museum, London, and Lund Humphries, London, 2016
2015	James Cahill and Maggi Hambling, *War Requiem and Afterm*ath, Unicorn Press, London, 2015

2001   John Berger, *Maggi and Henrietta*, Bloomsbury, London, 2001

2000   Robin Gibson and Norbert Lynton, *Painting the Century, 101 Portrait Masterpieces 1900–2000* (exh.cat.), National Portrait Gallery, London, and National Portrait Gallery Publications, London, 2000

1997   Martin Gayford, *British Figurative Art, Part One: Painting – The Human Figure* (exh.cat.), Flowers East, London, and Flowers Gallery Publications, London, 1997

1991   Mel Gooding, *Maggi Hambling – An Eye Through a Decade*, Yale Center for British Art, Newhaven, Connecticut, USA, 1991

1988   Barry Barker, *Moments of the Sun* (exh.cat.), Arnolfini Gallery, Bristol, 1988

1984   Richard Morphet, *The Hard-Won Image* (exh.cat.), Tate Gallery, London, and Tate Publishing, London, 1984

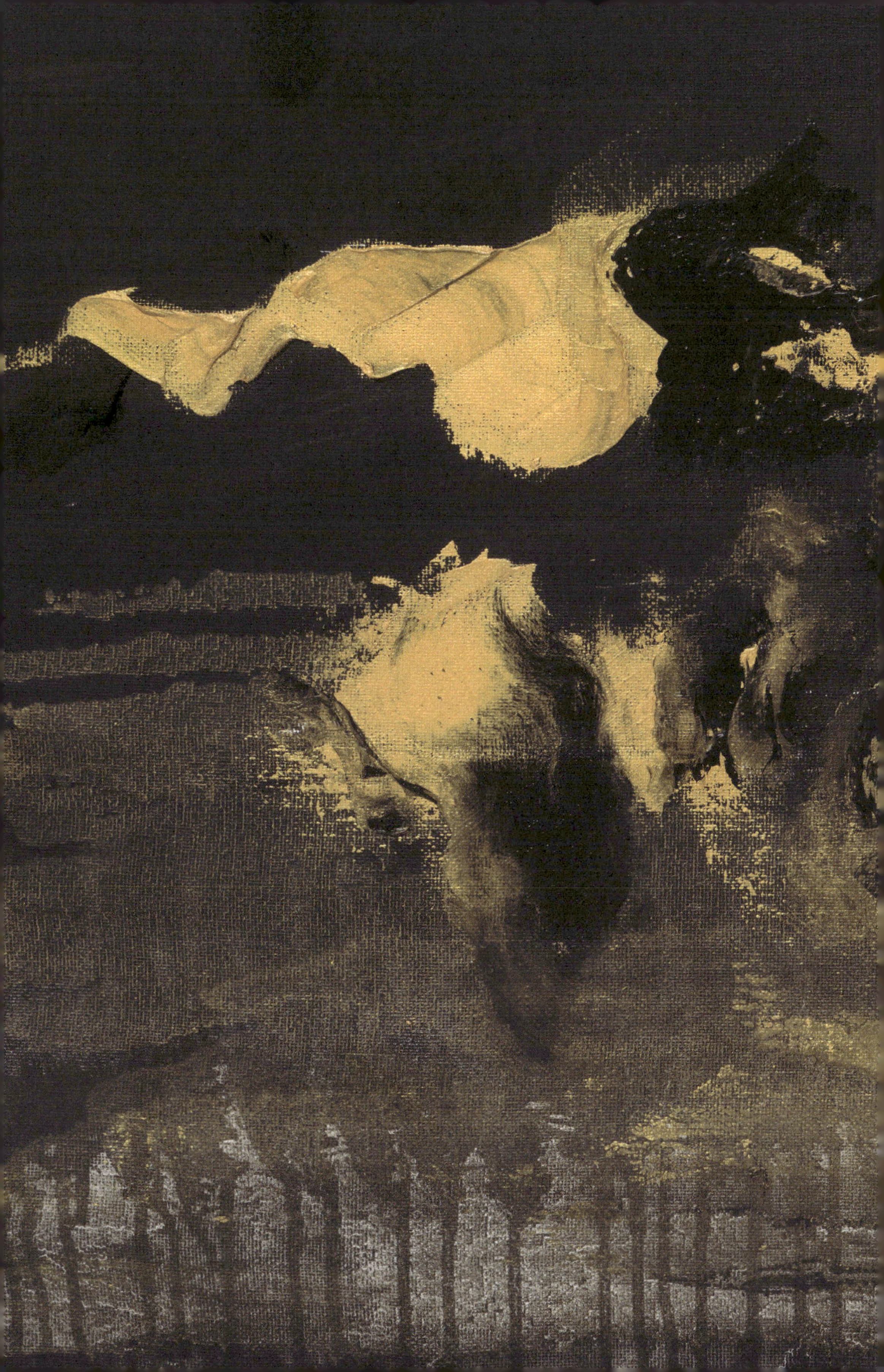

Acknowledgements

We would like to express our thanks to Hugh Monk and Frankie Rossi for their invaluable assistance.

Particular thanks are due to James Cahill and Sam Lee for their insightful essays; to Nick Cave and PJ Harvey for giving permission to reproduce their lyrics; and to Will Young for composing a piece for the exhibition. Also to Paul Britton who hosted the Singing With Nightingales evening that Maggi Hambling joined, inspiring the work in this exhibition. Our thanks are also due to the following managers and agents: Brian Message and Suzi Goodrich at ATC Management; Isobel Dixon and Finlay Charlesworth at Blake Friedmann Literary Agency Ltd; Joe Betts at BMG; Nickie Osborne at Hal Leonard Europe Limited; Adam Klein at Fascination Management; Sumit Bothra at SB3 Artist Management Ltd; Paul Burger and Nathy Cadlini at Soho Artists. Isabella Bragoli kindly provided assistance with image research, Douglas Atfield shot the penetrating portrait of Maggi Hambling and Ollie Denton captured the Singing With Nightingales events in his photographs.

We are grateful to all staff, trustees and volunteers at Pallant House Gallery, in particular our Chief Curator, Melanie Vandenbrouck, Curator, Miriam O'Connor Perks, and Registrar, Eleanor Chant, who managed the logistics of the exhibition and Nick Benham and team of art technicians for installing it so beautifully. Liv Nichols worked on all communications and David Wynn on the design.

This publication has been overseen by Harriet Olsen, Head of Publications, and we are grateful to the editor Susannah Worth, designers James and Brian Webb of Webb & Webb Design, and Gomer Press.

We are grateful to the Patrons of Pallant House Gallery and The Maggi Hambling Supporters Circle members, George and Jane Blunden; Tim Ashley and John Booth; Keith and Helen Clark; Marion Gibbs; and Frankie Rossi Art Projects, without whom this publication and the related exhibition would not have been possible.

But most of all, we could not have mounted this exhibition without the willingness and support of Maggi Hambling.